Crossing the Threshold

266 ways the State can enter your home

HARRY SNOOK

CENTRE FOR POLICY STUDIES
57 Tufton Street, London SW1P 3QL
2007

THE AUTHOR

HARRY SNOOK read Politics at the University of Durham, and afterwards worked for a Member of the European Parliament as an analyst on the EU's structural and cohesion policies. He later went on to study law, and is now a barrister.

Acknowledgements

Richard Smith, author of two previous CPS papers (*People, not budgets,* 2004, and *Charity*, 2006), was responsible for both the original idea and much of the background thinking for this report. In addition, support towards the research on which this report is based was given by the Institute for Policy Research.

ISBN No. 1 905389 50 7

Printed by 4 Print, 138 Molesey Avenue, Surrey

CONTENTS

SUMMARY

- Under English law, the citizen's home has traditionally been regarded as a privileged space. The courts have insisted that servants of the state cannot enter a private home without the occupier's permission unless a specific law authorises them to do so.
- Since the middle of the 20th century, the number of such legal provisions – powers of entry – has grown enormously, mirroring the expansion of the role of the state. There are now 266 powers allowing officials to enter a private home as of right.
- A number of these powers originate with European Union directives and regulations, rather than with an Act of Parliament passed by the UK's elected legislators.
- As a result of the proliferation and variety of entry powers, a citizen cannot realistically be aware of the circumstances in which his home may be entered by state officials without his consent, or what rights he has in such circumstances.
- Force can be used in the exercise of almost all these powers. In part this is due to its specific authorisation by law; in part to the courts' readiness to imply a right to use force on grounds of necessity.
- In many cases, discretion as to what is considered as reasonable behaviour in exercising an entry power is left to the judgement of those wielding the entry power.

- Many powers are drafted so broadly that the citizen has little or no protection if officials behave officiously or vindictively. Some carry draconian penalties for obstruction, including heavy fines and prison sentences of up to two years.

- Record-keeping by government agencies on how they use these powers is highly variable and sometimes seriously inadequate. For example, requests made under the Freedom of Information Act show that Her Majesty's Revenue and Customs keeps no regular record of the number of occasions on which its officers use the Writ of Assistance (one of the most intrusive and unregulated entry powers enjoyed by any state official).

Recommendations

- Entry powers are in serious need of reform. A new Act of Parliament should harmonise the procedural provisions of all existing entry powers and protect the citizen by making accountability and transparency paramount.

- Officials should always seek permission to enter a home if possible, even when they have a power to enter without it.

- A reasonable time for entry should be specified.

- With the exception of the emergency services, state officials should always have to get a warrant from a magistrate before they can force entry to a private home. The magistrate should carefully scrutinise their case and refuse a warrant where it is unnecessary.

- The exercise of entry powers should be thoroughly documented, and statistics on their use made public. This will put pressure on officials to use them in a reasonable and proportionate manner.

FOREWORD

by Professor Richard Stone

I AM VERY PLEASED to be able to write a Foreword to this paper. The subject of entry powers, and particularly of those other than the police and security services, has been of interest to me for nearly 30 years, ever since the decision in the House of Lords in the *Rossminster* case (*R v IRC, ex p Rossminster* [1980] AC 952) drew attention to the fact that many public authorities have powers to enter homes and business premises without permission. It prompted me to write a book attempting to catalogue and analyse the law relating to all powers entry (now in its fourth edition as *The Law of Entry, Search, and Seizure*, OUP, 2005). I am therefore full of admiration for the extensive work that has gone into this paper, identifying the range of powers which exist, and uncovering some which were new to me.

The section headed "A Day in the Life of a British Subject" is of particular importance. As well as illustrating the broad scope of the current powers, it vividly illustrates the fact that powers which may exist for perfectly reasonable purposes carry with them the possibility of oppressive use, unless they are properly constrained. Of course, the Human Rights Act 1998 means that public officials should only use their powers proportionately, if they are to avoid conflict with Article 8 of the European Convention on Human Rights (which protects privacy), but this only provides redress after the event, not protection beforehand. An entry on to premises, and the seizure of documents, may be very disruptive even if no further action follows. A much better approach is suggested here, with the use of a statutory framework for powers of entry. The police have to comply with the PACE Codes of Practice when exercising their powers; it is only reasonable that there should be similar constraints over the way in which other public officials exercise intrusive powers.

I very much hope that this paper, drawing attention to this important issue, will provide the catalyst for a long overdue regulation of an area where for too long the rights of the citizen have been put at the mercy of officials armed with powers which are not subject to proper control.

Professor Richard Stone
Lincoln Law School
University of Lincoln
March 2007

Professor Richard Stone is head of the Lincoln University Law School. Over the past 30 years he has taught at a variety of higher education institutions, including Leicester University (where he held the positions of Head of Department and Dean), Nottingham Trent University (where he was Dean of the Law School) and the Inns of Court School of Law (where he was Principal). He is the author of The Law of Entry, Search and Seizure *(4th Ed, Oxford University Press, 2005), the leading textbook on powers of entry.*

THE CONTEXT

by Jesse Norman

IN RECENT YEARS we have become used to news of police raids on crack dens and suspected terrorists. Open fields, however, are another matter. So one can only imagine the bemusement of local residents early on 10 January 2007 when a total of 22 people – including 10 government officials and 12 police officers – descended secretly and without notice on a remote field in Herefordshire. They erected a road block and used wire cutters to force their way in, without permission from the owners.

Who was the target of this police "hit"? Not a senior member of Al-Qaeda now living under an alias on a Herefordshire farm, alas. Not some ram-raiding jewel thieves sitting on a huge stash of swag. No – it was a nine-year old pet Jersey cow named Harriet, whom they wrongly suspected of having BSE.

If you want to learn more about Harriet, you will have to read this remarkable new pamphlet. But in so doing you will learn much else besides. The author has taken the little-understood but historically fundamental issue of the state's power to enter domestic premises, and used it as prism to shine new and revealing light on a huge range of current political issues and unresolved debates. The proper limits of state action, the privacy of individuals, the security of personal property, the nature of civic authority and administration, the growth of public bureaucracy, statute and regulation-all are illuminated by this brilliant essay.

The idea that an Englishman's home is his castle was famously given early expression in a different context by Sir Edward Coke, first Lord Chief Justice and framer of the Petition of Right (1628), in *The First Part of the Institutes of the Laws of England* of the same year. It was understood then that to cross the threshold of someone's property is to move from a public to a private world, a world in which, broadly, different social conventions, different moral obligations and different legal standards apply. Of course, the state has important reserved rights to enter homes in the public interest, rights that have expanded over time by democratic process, here as in other countries. But over the following three centuries it remained true in Britain that the home was enshrined by law and tradition as a zone free from state interference – somewhere to drop one's guard, to relax and to enjoy private family life.

It is the first achievement of this pamphlet to show how different matters are today: to clarify and catalogue the relevant law, and to describe how state powers to enter the home have grown over time. There are on the statute books in Britain today no fewer than 266 different laws allowing public authorities the right to enter private homes. Some require a warrant to be issued, some not; some require notice to be given, some not; some state the permissible hours of entry, some not; some carefully define the discretion of the entering person; some not. The overall picture is a mess of confused and intrusive regulation. The result is Harriet the cow and similar episodes; or more generally, a public culture obsessed with health and safety issues, huge government bureaucracy, endless pettifogging official intrusion into people's private lives, and – for obvious reasons – very little clear public understanding of the rights of the citizen.

As well as describing the problem, however, the author also makes a serious effort to solve it. His proposed reform would streamline and clarify the present body of law under three headings, geared to the nature of the public interest involved. And it would also insist on certain underlying principles, such as the need to ask permission before entering a property, or, failing that, to have a warrant; that warrants should always be independently scrutinised by a JP; and that proper records should always be kept. Many readers will be surprised that these principles are not already in place.

This is a balanced approach, which properly recognises the importance of the traditional British insistence that all entry powers should be individual ones. It constitutes a modest administrative reform, but one that would have a profound effect on the lives of many people over time. It thus deserves careful early consideration from all sides. Both the main political parties have contributed to the present situation. Both should take steps to remedy it.

Yet, to zoom out a little from the specifics, this essay also raises some important deeper questions. Harriet was not foreordained. It was not inevitable that we should have ended up with the present over-mighty official bureaucracy, and with ordinary citizens largely unaware of their rights and psychologically unempowered to act on them. Contrast the history of the US, in which the Fourth Amendment to the Constitution briefly and explicitly sets out a prohibition on unreasonable search of private premises and seizure of private property:

> *The right of the people to be secure in their persons, houses, papers, and effects, against unreasonable searches and seizures, shall not be violated, and no Warrants shall issue, but upon probable cause, supported by Oath or affirmation, and particularly describing the place to be searched, and the persons or things to be seized.*

That amendment was framed in part in reaction to the Crown's fondness for writs of assistance, open-ended search warrants that were used to search premises for tax purposes. Writs of assistance were abolished in the US by the Fourth Amendment. They remain on the statute book in this country today.

What has gone wrong here? A starting point is the heretical thought that this may be a specific area in which a new British Bill of Rights could strengthen the rights of the individual over and above those provided in the Human Rights Act.

However, we should also note the tension here between the general and the specific. It is like the Paradox of the Desk: every day it makes sense not to clear up your desk yet, but if you never clear it up the office ultimately grinds to a halt. Similarly, each individual statute may look reasonable on its face, each may properly reflect public concern as to a genuine social problem, and yet overall the unintended consequences can be deeply damaging. What makes the political case so difficult is the asymmetry involved. There is no constituency for the countless small benefits of a life lived freely. But every act of deregulation and citizen empowerment creates potential political risk, and so scope for public reaction if things go wrong. Imagine if Harriet had in fact contracted BSE by some unknown means. It would still have been lunacy to send in a SWAT team of officials and police. But don't put your money on the longevity of a politician who said so.

Our public culture thus undermines itself to some extent. It is often remarked that people today lack deference to others. This may be true in various walks of life. But as regards the state's power to enter your house, this pamphlet suggests the reverse: that in fact we have become far too deferential as a nation, far too willing to accept the dictates of faceless authority and of power wielded without public accountability. In the 18th Century, Britain was celebrated on the continent as the home of the liberty of the individual, of the theatre and the pub, a place where monarchical authority had been made subject to law and freethinkers could dissent more or less without reprisal. As Voltaire asked, why can't the laws that guarantee British liberties be adopted elsewhere? Today, the question almost sounds ironic.

Yet Voltaire's question had force, because it seemed to many then that the British had definitively answered Hobbes as to who, state or individual, was ultimately in charge. They had answered it in a typically British way, which fudged the status of the individual as between citizen and subject, and which deliberately blurred constitutional offices and functions. But at least they had done so, as the quarrelling powers of Europe had not, and would not for a century. The result was that, like Cromwell's russet-coated Captain, the British knew what they fought for, and loved what they knew.

What they fought for was the rule of law. Not laws as such, but the basic principles from which law springs. This pamphlet reminds us of some of those principles. As the issues of public against private power arise again – in the "rights to privacy" of celebrities who make their livings through publicity, in the curriculum and classroom practice of faith schools, in state funding for private religious adoption agencies, in the issuance of mandatory ID cards, in the balance between security and freedom in dealing with terrorism – we would do well to remember them. As well as Harriet.

Jesse Norman is Senior Fellow at Policy Exchange. He was previously a director at Barclays before leaving the City to research and teach at University College London. His books include The Achievement of Michael Oakeshott, Breaking the Habits of a Lifetime, *and* After Euclid. *His most recent book is* Compassionate Conservatism: What it is. Why we need it, *co-authored with Janan Ganesh (Policy Exchange, 2006).*

CHAPTER ONE

INTRODUCTION

The poorest man may in his cottage bid defiance to all the forces of the Crown. It may be frail, its roof may shake; the wind may blow through it; the storm may enter, the rain may enter – but the King of England cannot enter; all his force dares not cross the threshold of the ruined tenement.

William Pitt the Elder (1708-1778)

A man's house is his castle.

Sir Edward Coke (1552-1634)

THE SPECIAL STATUS of an individual's home as a place where their right to privacy and non-interference is elevated above other concerns has wide historic acceptance in political and legal culture.

A home is a place where the individual draws back from immediate participation in the formal community and assumes his natural, personal, family status. It is not just a different physical location to the street or the workplace, but an environment where the citizen can put aside their public role and in turn avoid the scrutiny and supervision which that role attracts. It is a sanctuary where we have a right to expect that we will be left alone unless there is a good reason to interfere with us.

When we step out of our houses and voluntarily enter the public space, we implicitly accept a level of supervision which we would not tolerate at home. Thus, the average individual is filmed dozens of times by CCTV cameras while on the street or using public transport, yet the use of such technology to routinely monitor our behaviour within the home is unthinkable. The state can monitor and control our streets, roads and shopping centres because it is its function to ensure orderly, lawful and proper conduct between citizens when they participate in the shared public space. Conversely, where our home life is concerned, the duties of the state are less and so, concomitantly, should be its powers. In a democracy, almost nobody suggests that we should be overseen in our living room to the same degree that we are outside.

At the other end of the spectrum, there are times when almost everyone would accept that the state does need to be able to enter citizens' private dwellings without their permission. This is especially the case when the need stems from the requirement to protect other citizens from harm. It goes without saying that fire and rescue services need to be able to enter homes without stopping to ask permission in an emergency. And where a serious crime has been or is about to be committed, it can be essential for the community that the police should be able to enter in order to counteract or prevent it.

But between these two extremes lie a multitude of situations in which the state may find it useful to enter a dwelling, but the social need for such powers is not so clear-cut. Are we happy for DEFRA inspectors to have the power to enter private land without consent? The answer may vary depending on whether they are taking steps to eradicate avian influenza, or whether they are just checking for the presence of foreign bees.

Of similar concern is the question of how such powers are to be exercised – what kind of rights a householder has to object to entry or contest it, and what can be done against him if he refuses to allow it. The less the circumstances of the entry resemble an emergency, the greater the citizen's expectation that he will be told in advance and perhaps allowed to lodge an appeal against the planned encroachment. It thus seems reasonable that when a gas supplier wishes to enter private land in order to find out if it is suitable to have gas stored under it, the occupier must be given 28 days' notice. It may appear less so when, under the Gas Act 1965, the inspector can obtain a magistrate's warrant to force entry and the householder can be fined for obstructing him. In such circumstances it is the behaviour of those wielding such powers that determines whether their effect is to correctly discharge the duties of the state, or to oppress and harass the citizen.

CHAPTER TWO

WHAT IS A POWER OF ENTRY?

A POWER OF ENTRY IS a right, established by law, to enter private property without the consent of the owner or occupier. The focus of this paper is on those entry powers that provide officials of bodies carrying out a public function – such as central government, local authorities and utilities companies – with the right to enter a citizen's home or his private land.

English law has never countenanced the idea that state officials should have sweeping, general powers to do something so potentially oppressive as entering a citizen's home without his consent. Therefore there is no single, overarching legal power of public servants, be they police officers or pensions inspectors, to enter private property. If they are to effect such an entry, they must be able to rely upon a specific law that authorises them to do so in particular circumstances.

If such a law does not exist or does not apply in the circumstances in which an official wishes to use it, any entry to private property without the permission of the occupier will be unlawful and an act of trespass,[1] for which the official may be sued by the occupier. It is immaterial whether the entry was authorised by a senior civil servant or a minister, or whether it was an important step in carrying out the official's duties: without a specific entry power found somewhere in the law, the official is a

---

1 Unless it is for the purpose of saving life and limb, or preventing damage to property, in which case permission will be "implied by necessity".

trespasser just as a private citizen would be on walking into another's house unbidden and uninvited. This principle has been unambiguously enshrined in English law since the middle of the eighteenth century, when the Lord Chief Justice ruled in the case of *Entick v Carrington*[2] that officers sent by a cabinet minister to search a subject's house had acted illegally, because there was no entry power to be found in statute on which they could rely.

The fact that all entry powers are individual has led to a widespread divergence in their wording and procedural requirements. Analysis of those powers catalogued in the Appendix to this paper shows how little consistency there is in the form and nature of entry powers. The following are a few of the areas in which this diversity is manifested:

- 26% of powers provide for notice of intended entry to be given to the occupier. Of these, 56% require 24 hours' notice, 6% 48 hours, 14% 7 days, 1.5% 10 days, 11% 14 days, 1.5% 21 days and 9% 28 days.

- 34% of powers provide that the person exercising it must show their authority if asked.

- 24% require that the power be exercised at a reasonable time.

- Of the 25% of powers allowing for a warrant to be obtained, 77% specify that the warrant authorises the use of force, leaving this to be inferred by the courts in the case of the remaining 23%. In cases where a warrant must be obtained before entry, 64% of establishing laws make clear that force can be used.

---

2 See Chapter 4. Source: (1765) 19 Howell's state Trials 1030.

- Of the 31% of powers carrying penalties for obstruction, fines range from £20 (1%) through £200 (27%), £500 (19%), £1,000 (3%), £2,500 (8%) to £5,000 on summary conviction (43%), while under another 6%, obstruction can carry a prison sentence.

While it is arguable that this specificity has allowed the legislature to tailor the form of each power to suit its purpose, such great variety leaves the citizen in a state of uncertainty with regard to the state's power to invade his home. Unless he is a lawyer, he is unable to predict reliably the behaviour of the state's officials when they wish to effect an entry; leaving him uncertain about the degree of notice to which he is entitled, whether and to whom he can contest the entry, and what might be done against him if he tries to prevent it happening.

One possible reform to the law of entry would be to bring all powers under a single Act. This would provide for a simpler set of universal rules regarding entry with which the citizen would find it much easier to familiarise himself. In a situation where entry to his property was contemplated or underway, he would be able to fall back on a set of basic rules which he would know applied in all circumstances.

For this improvement to take effect it would not be necessary to reduce all powers to a single form. A small number of classes of powers, each exhibiting internal consistency, would go a long way to achieving the same result while recognising the need identified above for different levels of safeguards applying to different powers. As will be shown, there is evidence that the legislature and the statutory draftsmen who prepare Bills have attempted over the centuries to use similar wording for similar powers, and the resulting statutory provisions can be grouped into a number of rough categories. However, it is clear that the level of consistency within these categories is deeply unsatisfactory.

CHAPTER THREE

THE PROLIFERATION OF ENTRY POWERS

THE NUMBER OF POWERS OF entry in force has increased substantially from the middle of the twentieth century onwards. Powers of entry are frequently introduced as an enforcement mechanism in legislation regulating the activities of the state in running public services or in supervising the activities of the population. As the state's level of participation in society and national life has grown, so has the number of Acts of Parliament regulating that participation, and with it the number of entry powers.

The growth in powers of entry should therefore be seen in context as a symptom of the expanding role of the state in the lives of citizens. During the last century, the degree to which the individual interacted involuntarily with the state vastly increased. As A J P Taylor noted, before the First World War, the average citizen's interaction with the government was largely limited to paying tax:[3]

> *Until August 1914 a sensible, law-abiding Englishman could pass through life and hardly notice the existence of the state, beyond the post office and the policeman. He could live where he liked and as he liked. He had no official number or identity card. He could travel abroad or leave his country for ever without a passport or any sort of official permission. He could exchange his money for any other currency without restriction or limit. He could buy goods from any country in the world on the same terms as he bought goods at home.*

---

[3] A J P Taylor, *English History, 1914-1945,* Oxford University Press, 1965.

Today, the situation is very different. Pensions, wages, healthcare, vehicle maintenance, childcare and child support, broadcasting and the receipt of broadcasts; all activities in which the state now has an active interest and a relationship with the citizen which would have been inconceivable a few generations ago. And in each of the fields mentioned above, the state has supported its new role by enacting new powers of entry.

The state's motives for extending its influence over the lives of the populace are often beneficent, seeking to improve the lives of its subjects by binding them into the framework of the welfare state and, more broadly, by regulating their behaviour for their own protection. However, this benign interventionism has come at a civic cost. As early as the 19th century, liberal thinkers such as Herbert Spencer were already identifying the stifling effect of the increasingly maternal state on the citizen's capacity for autonomy and self-improvement.[4] And in the present day, the vast and perplexing variety of entry powers is one source of concern about the growth of a "surveillance society", shortly to be the subject of a Parliamentary inquiry.

The indigenous development of the interventionist state has been accompanied by the appearance of a new supranational source of regulation unforeseen in Spencer's day. The institutions of the European Union today exercise a large influence over the development of the law and the activities of government in the United Kingdom. In addition to the numerous Acts of Parliament whose passage is motivated by the need to comply with EU directives, this influence takes a more direct effect through regulations issued by ministers under the European Communities Act. British citizens can now find their lives and livelihoods subjected to forms of supervision enacted not by their own elected Parliament, but by ministers implementing the will of EU bodies. This paper

---

4 See H Spencer, *The Man Versus The State*, 1884.

documents 12 powers of entry into the private homes of British citizens which have been introduced into English law in this manner.

The overall effect of the proliferation of entry powers which has accompanied the expansion of the state's role in the lives of its citizens is to cause its relationship with them to be carried out increasingly on the state's terms. The large number of entry powers not only means that the citizen is far more susceptible to having his home entered by the state's agents than before, but that their great variety and inconsistency mean that he cannot realistically be aware of their form and extent.

The expansion of entry powers

The state's armoury of entry powers continues to expand unabated. Taking only the powers catalogued in the Appendix to this paper – that is to say, powers which are currently in force and which permit entry to private dwellings – it can swiftly be seen at what a high rate Parliament produces new powers. Thirty-one of the current statutory powers were enacted during the 1970s, 62 during the 1980s and a further 67 during the 1990s. The actual figures for the number of powers enacted in a given decade will inevitably be higher, since those given do not include powers which have subsequently been repealed or replaced.[5]

---

[5] The dates of enactment of the powers listed in the Appendix to this paper exhibit a clear trend for a continuing decade-upon-decade increase in the number of such laws being passed, with particularly sharp upturns in the 1960s and 1980s. However, this does not of course take into account the possibility that powers which once existed might have been repealed or replaced. To have searched for and counted such historic powers would have been beyond the scope of this study due to the methodological complications of searching repealed or amended Acts in their original wording. The author's experience in researching the subject is, however, that it is very rare for any power of entry to be repealed without its being simultaneously replaced by an updated equivalent. There is therefore good reason to believe that the issue of repealed Acts would not significantly affect the identified trend of increase.

So far, the first decade of the 21st century has seen 25 new statutory entry powers enacted, and at the time of writing, a bill is being put forward which will see further very broad powers added to the list. The Tribunals, Courts and Enforcement Bill contains provisions harmonising the rules concerning bailiffs and their powers to seize and sell debtors' property. In an example of the broad drafting which leaves the citizen uncertain of his rights, Paragraph 7 (2) of Schedule 12 to the Bill leaves it up to a government minister to make regulations concerning how much notice needs to be given, what it must state and how it must be sent. It is also left to a minister to decide whether there should be any restrictions on re-entering premises multiple times (Paragraph 14 (3)).

Paragraphs 17 and 20 provide that the bailiff may use reasonable force to break into premises, and Paragraph 24 (2) allows a minister to make regulations allowing the use of violence against persons during the entry. Under Paragraph 27, the bailiff may take with him any number of other people (who do not have to be bailiffs or police officers), and they can also use any degree of force that the bailiff is entitled to. Paragraph 25 requires that entry be effected "at a prescribed time of day", but does not require that this time be reasonable. If anyone obstructs the bailiff, they face a fine of £2,500 and up to a year in prison under Paragraph 68 (3).

The broad drafting of the Bill and its Schedules, and its failure to provide concrete standards for the activities of bailiffs, instead leaving their regulation largely to a Minister, shows how the problems of arbitrariness and uncertainty are still very much current.

CHAPTER FOUR

CASE STUDY 1
ENTICK v CARRINGTON

THE ENGLISH jurisprudential tradition has for centuries provided the citizen with a significant measure of protection against the arbitrary power of the state. When the issue of entry powers was first litigated, the courts' insistence on the rule of law ensured that the citizen's home was safe against all intrusion except that mandated specifically by Parliament or by the known common law. However, as this case study illustrates, the protective effect of this principle has been compromised by the enormous growth in such laws.

On 11 November 1762, four officers employed by the Secretary of State for the Northern Department (a position analogous to today's Home Secretary) broke into the house of John Entick in Stepney. Over the course of the next four hours the officers, led by one Nathan Carrington, proceeded to ransack the house, breaking open boxes, cabinets and drawers, forcing locks and smashing down interior doors. Having caused damage estimated at £2,000 (then a very large sum), the intruders finally left, taking with them many of Mr Entick's possessions, especially his private papers.

John Entick was a publisher, and the Secretary of State had sent his men to seize evidence that he had been involved in producing *The North Briton*, a radical newspaper founded by John Wilkes which had made veiled attacks on King George III's foreign policy, and on his political integrity. The authorities were particularly angered by an edition which strongly hinted that the King had lied during a speech. Mr Entick's home was broken into and his belongings taken in order to find evidence of the crime of seditious libel.

When Entick sued Carrington and the other officers for trespass, the Defendants relied upon their "warrant", which was not a JP's order like the warrants issued under modern legislation, but in fact amounted to no more than an "authorisation" from the Secretary of State. Although Parliament had enacted no law giving the Secretary of State the power to authorise his officers to force their way into subjects' homes for this purpose, the Defendants claimed that as a government official responsible for internal security, he implicitly enjoyed an inherent power to order such action. The Lord Chief Justice, Lord Camden, utterly rejected this assertion and found in Mr Entick's favour, his decision establishing the principle that entry powers can only exist when they have been specifically provided by legislation or the common law.

More than 240 years later, such legislation exists in such vast quantities that any officer in Mr Carrington's position would be highly unlikely to need to rely on the precarious notion of an implicit power.

Imagine that the year is 2007, and that the satirical website northbriton.com has accused the Prime Minister of lying over his foreign policy decisions. Although the authorities might be anxious to disrupt webmaster Entick's operations, they can no longer claim an "implicit right" to force their way into his house. However, seditious libel is still a criminal offence under English law, carrying a possible sentence of life imprisonment. Proving that what was said is true affords no defence. Because of the long prison sentence available, seditious libel would qualify as an "arrestable offence" under the Police and Criminal Evidence Act 1984. The police would therefore be able to force entry in order to arrest Entick. Even if they lacked sufficient evidence to arrest him immediately, they could get a search warrant under the same legislation, entitling them to break in and rifle through his belongings in much the same way as their predecessors did illegally in 1762. All they would need to do is convince a magistrate that there are reasonable grounds for believing that evidence of seditious libel was on the premises, that Entick either would not let them in or would destroy the evidence if warned, and that his behaviour threatened "serious harm to the security of the state or to public order".[6]

If webmaster Entick were to criticise strongly uncontrolled immigration, things would be worse. A warrant under the Public Order Act 1986 would allow his home to be searched for any evidence of "racially inflammatory material". And should his criticism of the Prime Minister's foreign policy lead him to suggest that British servicemen refuse their orders, the Home Secretary's men would be back to search again under the Incitement to Disaffection Act 1934.

The authorities might well run up against an objection under the Human Rights Act, on the grounds that their activities would unnecessarily deprive webmaster Entick of his rights to free expression and respect for his home and family life. Yet the law remains, and by the time Entick could raise any such objection, his premises would have been broken into and his belongings taken.

Today, the authorities could also quite easily disrupt the webmaster's operations using regulatory powers. If northbriton.com has employees, webmaster Entick could soon find his premises being turned over by inspectors from the Department of Work and Pensions, acting under the Social Security Administration Act 1992, the National Minimum Wage Act 1998 or the Pensions Act 1995. Was that a tobacco advert on the website's front page? Back come the Inspectors with a warrant to search webmaster Entick's premises for evidence of promoting smoking. And if any of his publications referenced sexual or violent themes, the police could break in once more under the Children and Young Persons (Harmful Publications) Act 1955 or the Obscene Publications Act 1959.

In 1762, Carrington was liable for trespass because he had acted without a statutory authorisation for his violent entry onto Mr Entick's premises. Today, his biggest problem would be deciding which Act to choose.

---

6 Police and Criminal Evidence Act 1984, s 115 (6).

CHAPTER FIVE

CASE STUDY 2: HARRIET THE COW

THE PROLIFERATION AND VARIETY OF ENTRY POWERS is not the only way in which the current state of the law fails to afford adequate protection to the citizen. Many of the procedural requirements for entry are drafted broadly, and assume a substantial level of professionalism, politeness and proportionate behaviour on the part of the officials wielding the power. While the majority of public servants exhibit these qualities, the following case study shows how broad drafting leaves the citizen defenceless when individual officials suffer a failure of common sense.

Herefordshire couple David Price and Liz Davis are the owners of a nine-year-old Jersey cow named Harriet. Harriet was bought as a present for the couple's son, and has spent her entire life as a domestic pet.

Unfortunately for Harriet, she had been brought up on a farm where another cow had contracted Bovine Spongiform Encephalopathy – BSE or "Mad Cow Disease". Under a European Union directive, cows which are at risk of exposing the public to BSE must be destroyed, and officials from the Department of Environment, Food and Rural Affairs (DEFRA) notified Mr Price and Ms Davis that they had decided to slaughter Harriet.

The family protested that the EU directive was aimed at cattle who would enter the food chain, whereas Harriet was a beloved family pet who was never going to be slaughtered for meat. They pointed out that written records showed that she had never had contact with, or shared food with, the infected cow. The

Department was insistent however, and when the family appealed to the courts, DEFRA fought the case all the way to the House of Lords, which eventually ruled in the Department's favour.

After intervention by the local MP, Mark Harper, a DEFRA minister promised that Harriet would be given a "stay of execution" until a judge had reviewed the case. But at 9:30am on 10 January 2007, a team of 22 people, including 10 government officials and 12 police officers, swooped on Harriet's field, without any advance warning having been given. The "hit squad" had erected a road block to seal off the area, and used bolt-cutters to force their way into the enclosure. Harriet's life was saved only by the family and a group of locals who rushed to the scene to confront the intruders after a tip-off. The DEFRA officials and their escort backed down, and Harriet's case is now the subject of a judicial review in the High Court. If the tip-off had not been made, Harriet would have been slaughtered and her carcass removed before the family knew anything about it.

The actions taken by the Department's inspectors – arriving secretly, in large numbers, without notice and accompanied by police, and breaking into private property with bolt cutters – may seem extreme. The family had always resisted the slaughter of Harriet by legitimate, legal means such as appealing to the courts and contacting their MP. Yet there was no suggestion that they would assault DEFRA inspectors acting in pursuance of their duties. So why did the Department feel it necessary to send 12 police officers? Nobody alleged that Harriet would be spirited away, so why did the team arrive secretly, early in the morning? While these concerns relate to the decisions taken by individual inspectors and their managers, a more significant issue is that the powers of state officials in this area permit just this sort of behaviour.

There can be no doubt that the inspectors were behaving legally. The Transmissible Spongiform Encephalopathies Regulations 2006, which implement European Union rules on dealing with BSE, provide that:

- Inspectors can force their way onto private land without the occupier's consent, without having to get a magistrate's warrant. They therefore have no need to prove to any independent person that they have good reasons for their actions.
- Inspectors can enter premises at any reasonable time, but since they do not need to seek a warrant from an independent magistrate, it is up to them to decide what is a "reasonable time".
- Domestic premises may be entered if necessary.
- Inspectors can take with them such other persons as they consider necessary. Again, it is up to the inspectors to determine what is necessary, so they can take a team of 22 people including 12 police officers if they decide they are needed.
- A European Commission official supervising the enforcement of EU regulations and directives can accompany the inspectors.
- An official entering under these regulations has wide powers to seize and dispose of any animal or part of an animal, to carry out "any inquiries, investigations, examinations and tests", to force the owner of the animals to round them up, and to lock up any container or store.
- The regulations give all officials acting under them blanket immunity from any personal liability arising from their actions, even if they were only "purporting" to carry out their duties.
- Contrasting with the absolute legal protection afforded to inspectors, anyone "obstructing" an inspector (such as the crowd of local people who arrived to protect Harriet) can be fined £5,000 or even sent to prison for up to two years.

We have clearly come a long way from the idea that an Englishman's home is his castle. And yet few Englishmen have been asked whether they are happy with the powers now accrued by the state.

CHAPTER SIX

WHEN CAN FORCE BE USED IN THE EXERCISE OF AN ENTRY POWER?

ALTHOUGH A DEFINITIVE CASE on the issue has not emerged from English jurisprudence, a number of judgments have established that an entry to premises is "forcible" whenever the entrant applies any physical force to any part of the structure in order to gain access without the permission of the occupier. This could be as little as pushing open a door, even one that is already ajar,[7] or turning a key in a lock.[8] Where an entry power confers no right to use force, it therefore follows that an officer acting in its exercise is entitled to do no more than walk onto land and into buildings whose doors are open wide enough to let him pass through.

Perhaps because of the tight restrictions imposed on the behaviour of entrants which this definition implies, the courts have been ready to infer that force may be used in support of a wide variety of entry powers. Of course, there are many statutes that specifically grant entry powers accompanied by a right to use "reasonable force", but when the establishing law is silent on the issue, the courts have often found that the use of force is to be implied by necessity. Officials of local and central government agencies can therefore often use force to enter a private home, even when Parliament never explicitly authorised such behaviour in the statute granting the power.

---

7 *Swales v Cox* [1981] QB 849.

8 *Re: Calf and Sun Insurance Office* [1920] 2 KB 366.

Generally, if the power is in a form where a warrant is available, the courts will infer that the warrant must be obtained in order for force to be used. Any warrant will normally be interpreted as authorising the use of force, even if the statute under which it is issued does not mention it.

In summary, officials may use force in support of a power of entry when:

a) the statutory source of the power makes mention of the use of force and establishes when it can be employed; or,

b) the statutory source of the power does not explicitly exclude force, force may nonetheless be used if there is nobody on the property; or, if entry is refused,

c) a warrant is available, even if the text of the statute does not specify that the warrant authorises force. To balance this, force may not be used without a warrant if a warrant can be obtained.

CHAPTER SEVEN

CLASSES OF ENTRY POWERS

WHILE EACH LAW establishing a power of entry is individual, the powers considered by this paper exhibit a range of "severity". This includes variations in the immediacy of force, in the notice period, and in the requirement for a JP's warrant.

Category one: where force can be used immediately

A number of entry powers provide that an officer or official may enter a dwelling immediately, using reasonable force if it is necessary to do so. The majority of these powers have a clear "emergency" character, and are designed to be used in the course of law enforcement, firefighting or the protection of the public from severe environmental or industrial dangers such as malfunctioning electrical plant or extremely hazardous pollution.

Police powers allowing immediate forcible entry are generally targeted at situations where the public is at immediate risk of harm, or where the entry is for purposes related to the arrest of a suspect for a serious offence.

In each of these cases, there is a clear argument in favour of dispensing with procedural safeguards in favour of rapid action. When life and limb are genuinely and immediately threatened, the potential harm to the citizen from delay is greater than the harm done by the setting aside of his right to privacy and to respect for his property. If we accept that the most fundamental duty of the state is to protect its people, then it follows that there are circumstances in which a failure to enter private property immediately would severely compromise its ability to discharge that duty.

However, some entry powers in the "immediate force" category do not seem to be justified on these grounds. For example, certain customs officers hold a long-term authorisation known as a "writ of assistance". The writ of assistance allows its holder to bypass the normal safeguards on the behaviour of customs officials, who are otherwise required to obtain a warrant from a Justice of the Peace (JP) before effecting a forcible entry to a dwelling. A writ of assistance is not limited to a specific investigation or purpose, but can be uised whenever it is considered necessary by HMRC managers. It is not time-limited, but is valid for the entirety of the reign of the monarch in which it is issued, potentially a period of many decades. An officer holding such a writ can break into a private house in order to seize any goods which he believes are liable to be forfeited to Her Majesty's Revenue & Customs (HMRC), without justifying this action to any independent judicial authority beforehand.

It appears that Parliament has recognised the uncommonly severe nature of this power, as it made a gesture at restraining it in the Finance Act 2000. This provided that an officer with a Writ of Assistance should normally still obtain a JP's warrant in the normal way, unless the goods to be seized are likely to be removed, destroyed or lost before this can be done. However, the decision on whether this "danger" is so great that entry should be forced without the permission of a JP is left to the officer holding the writ. The so-called restriction therefore amounts to little more than an admonition that such an officer should ask first, if he thinks he can spare the time.

In such a case, the competition of interests is not one of the citizen's safety versus the citizen's privacy; as in the case of entry for firefighting or lifesaving purposes. Instead, it is between the citizen's privacy and the state's financial interests. This is self-evidently a different situation from one in which a person is threatened with physical harm. The argument can be coherently made that where civil rights are to be abrogated in order to assist the state rather than to protect the citizen, forcible entry without prior judicial oversight is much less acceptable. The reform in the Finance Act 2000 was an acknowledgement of this, but it shied away from abolishing the Writ of Assistance, as has been officially proposed or enacted in other common law jurisdictions.[9]

The first request under the Freedom of Information Act

As part of the research undertaken for this study, we used the Freedom of Information Act to ask HMRC for statistics on the use of the Writ of Assistance. We requested figures on the number of times during the last full year on which an officer holding a Writ of Assistance had exercised his right to effect entry by force without obtaining a magistrates' warrant. HMRC told us that:[10]

> *Unfortunately, HMRC does not routinely record the number of times that the power [...] is used, and consequently does not hold the information in the form that you requested.*

However, HMRC did divulge the results of a "statistical exercise" carried out in 2004/05, which showed that during that year, entry had been effected under a Writ of Assistance on 102 occasions, with a 75% "success rate", although no details were given on the definition of "success" in this context.

HMRC pointed out that the figure of 102 searches of private property without a JP's supervision was lower than that found by a previous "statistical exercise" carried out in 1978/9, when 537 searches under Writ were counted. However, this is likely to be of little comfort to the occupiers of the 102 private premises entered by Customs officers without notice and without any independent supervision or accountability; especially to the 25% against whom no evidence was found.

---

9 The Fourth Amendment to the Constitution of the United States of America outlaws Writs of Assistance. Canada has also proposed their abolition: see Law Reform Commission of Canada, Report 19, *Writs of Assistance and Telewarrants,* 1983, 44.

10 Letter from HMRC dated 15 March 2007, reference FOI 1148/07.

A further request under the Freedom of Information Act revealed that the number of Writs of Assistance in force has grown rapidly over the last two years, with 196 currently in force, compared to 125 in 2005.[11]

Regardless of whether or not one accepts the arguments in favour of the continued existence of the Writ of Assistance in its current form, it is certainly one of the most broad and most arbitrary entry powers in force, and one of the least susceptible to independent scrutiny before its exercise. In recognition of this, its use ought at least to be documented with a rigour and thoroughness proportionate to its oppressive potential; transparency being at its most vital when the state's intrusive power is at its most absolute.

It is surely unacceptable that the agency responsible for exercising the power does not even document its use except for a "statistical exercise" which appears to be carried out at an interval of a quarter of a century.

Category two: powers where a JP's warrant must be obtained before entering

Some powers require that a warrant be sought before entry can be effected. The large number of powers set out in this form usually relate to the detection and control of activities which are illegal, usually in a commercial context. For example, there are powers to inspect for the sale of knives in violation of the Knives Act 1997, to check for criminal copyright infringement, or to search for an unlicensed television. The powers of the police to effect immediate entry would not apply to these activities however, either because they do not pose a risk to the safety of members of the public, or because the inspection is to discover whether an infraction is being committed, rather than to arrest someone whom there is reason to suspect has been guilty of it. These powers can therefore be

[11] Letter from HMRC dated 12 April 2007, reference FOI 1227/07.

broadly characterised as being aimed at matters whose severity places them between the "regulatory" issues and "law enforcement" powers.

An official applying for a warrant to execute one of these powers will normally have to give evidence before a JP to show reasons why the power should be carried out.

Category three: powers where entry can be effected without a warrant, but a warrant can be obtained

A large body of entry powers are phrased in such a way that the beneficiary is entitled to enter immediately into a private dwelling without obtaining a warrant from a JP, but has the option to obtain such a warrant if necessary. The numerous powers following this form are nearly all regulatory in character, being used to inspect agricultural produce and farming practices, planning and housing matters, surveys for the purposes of planning utilities infrastructure, compliance with pensions regulations and other such issues.

Where a power is phrased in this way, an officer exercising it is entitled to enter onto private premises as of right, without asking permission. He or she can walk onto and over land and into open buildings, carrying out any inspections and removing any samples or evidence that the particular law in question allows or requires.

Because of the option to obtain a warrant, courts have usually interpreted such powers as providing that any entry without a warrant must not involve the use of force. Thus, an inspector acting without a warrant could not overpower someone blocking their route onto the land, nor could they break down a door or force a window to enter a house, even while the occupier was away. As noted in the description of "force" above, this does not mean that permission is needed in order to effect entry. Additionally, the wording of many powers leaves open the possibility that any householder preventing entry without a warrant could be fined for obstruction.

Where a warrant can be obtained, the law usually specifies that the warrant authorises the recipient to use reasonable force, or such reasonable force as is necessary to carry out his or her duties. Sometimes (particularly in older Acts) the law is silent on the use of force with a warrant, but the courts are usually willing to infer that force is available, or there would be no reason for Parliament to have provided for a warrant to be obtainable.

Category four: where there is no mention of force, and no warrant available

A large number of laws enact entry powers without any provision for a warrant to be obtained, but (unlike those in Category One) do not state that the officials exercising the power may use force. Powers falling into this category tend to be of a very mild regulatory nature such as inspections of riding establishments, or to be unconnected with any control of the occupier's behaviour, as in the case of the provisions allowing Revenue officers to cross private land in order to access a pipeline.

The second request under the Freedom of Information Act

Even when they might be thought obscure, powers falling into this category are exercised with surprising frequency. Using the Freedom of Information Act, we asked the DEFRA for figures on the use of the power of entry contained in the Bees Act 1980. The Act provides that inspectors may enter private land in order to inspect bee colonies for disease or for the presence of foreign species of bee. No warrant is available or needed, and entry can be exercised immediately.

To its credit, DEFRA responded promptly (within a day) and fully.[12] Their figures showed that during 2006, 3,190 apiaries were inspected in England, and a further 940 in Wales. While DEFRA's statistics apply to all types of land, they readily estimated that "the

---

12 Letter from DEFRA dated 22 February 2007, reference PHE 2084.

vast majority of inspections carried out (99%+) take place on privately owned property". The detail of its record-keeping for this essentially harmless power contrasts markedly with the failure of HMRC to account for its use of Writs of Assistance.

From the wording of these statutory provisions, it could easily be thought that they could not be used forcibly. However, as will be seen, the courts have been ready to find an implicit right to use force under certain circumstances, partially compensating for the non-availability of a warrant without providing for the oversight that a warrant application brings.

It can be seen that there is a rough but clear correlation between the degree to which a citizen's liberty stands to be threatened by entry onto his property, and the degree of restraint imposed by the law on the power's exercise. In general, the greater the punitive or oppressive potential of an entry power, the stronger the requirement for its beneficiary to obtain approval from an independent figure. For example, the most intrusive surveillance powers such as those under the Police Act 1997 require authorisation by a specialist senior judge; while a routine regulatory inspection under the Riding Establishments Act 1964 does not even have to be approved by a magistrate. Where the citizen's interests are actually dependent on the exercise of the entry power, in such cases as an intervention by the fire brigade or by emergency pollution control teams, safeguards such as notice periods and warrants can be dispensed with altogether.

This makes sense. Most citizens would agree that they would want the highest level of judicial supervision when the state's actions were at their most intrusive and where the potential consequences at their most severe for the property's occupier. However, it is questionable whether such safeguards should be dispensed with altogether when the entry power exists for routine and trivial purposes. That officials cannot plant bugging devices in my home without a judge's say-so is reassuring; that they can forcibly enter my land without permission or any independent oversight in order to take samples of fertiliser is not.

Furthermore, the correlation is spoilt by a significant number of aberrant powers, whose level of safeguarding does not match their intrusive nature. Examples include the Writ of Assistance discussed earlier, and the extremely broad power in the Housing Act 1985 which allows officials to enter any council house at any time, without restraint. If citizens are to have the reassurance of knowing that the state's power to enter their homes will be circumscribed and supervised in proportion to its severity, such anomalies must be ironed out.

CHAPTER EIGHT

ANATOMY OF AN ENTRY POWER

DESPITE THE WIDE VARIETY and inconsistency in the drafting of powers of entry, there are a number of features common to the vast majority of the statutory provisions that establish them. As a rule, powers of entry are phrased in a manner which specifies:

- what categories of persons are eligible to exercise the power. For example, the entry power under Section 5 of the Knives Act 1997 is exercisable by "a constable", while that under Section 97 of the Local Government and Housing Act 1989 is to be used by "a person authorised by the local housing authority or the Secretary of State".
- what kind of premises can be entered. Some entry powers aimed at regulating commercial activities preclude entry to "premises used only as a dwelling", but allow a person's home to be entered if it is used for any business purpose. Others simply refer to "any premises".
- for what purpose the entry is to be effected. Sometimes this can be quite specific, but many powers are phrased broadly in this regard. For example, Section 40 (1) (b) of the Countryside and Rights of Way Act 2000 allows entry to be effected "for the purpose of determining whether any power conferred on the appropriate countryside body [...] should be exercised in relation to the land".

This "who, where, why" structure is the basic minimum needed to establish a power of entry in statute. Many powers however – and especially those enacted more recently – are drafted so as to specify other procedural forms or requirements that must be adhered to. These include:

- whether the official must show any documentation to the occupier when entering, such as a "document showing his authority".
- how much, if any, notice must be given to the owner or occupier of the premises before entry can be effected.
- whether a warrant can or must be sought, the preconditions for its grant and what the warrant allows.
- at what times officials can exercise the power.
- whether or not force can be used.
- what actions the official can take once on the premises, possibly including removing samples or documents.
- whether it is a criminal offence to obstruct the official exercising the power, and what penalty it carries.

Authorisations

The text of many of the statutes establishing entry powers provide that an officer exercising them may enter premises "on the production of some duly authenticated document showing his authority", sometimes adding that this obligation arises only where the occupier asks to see it.

The "authority" referred to means no more than that the officer has been chosen to wield the particular power of entry that is proposed to be used. For example, many entry powers are expressed as being available to "an officer of a local authority authorised in writing". The "authority" that would need to be shown in such a case would merely be a statement from the Council that it has designated the officer carrying it to carry out the entry. It is not therefore a legal document, still less evidence that the power is being used properly or appropriately.

However, the presence of such a document does provide the occupier of the entered premises with some level of reassurance. He or she will be able to see the name of the inspector standing on the doorstep, and the identity and nature of the agency employing him. Such knowledge is important for the proper regulation of entry powers, since it will be vital information for any complaint or legal action to be raised after the entry has been effected.

Notice

Except in relation to powers which have a "law enforcement" flavour, or those which are to be effected by surprise in order to prevent the destruction or concealment of evidence, there is a general tendency to require inspectors to give householders notice before they enter their home. There is usually no prescribed form for the notice, which can take the form of a simple letter.

More importantly, there is no consistency whatsoever regarding the amount of notice that must be given to a householder. One can find acts requiring notice of 28 days, 14 days, 10 days, 7 days, 48 hours or even as little as 24 hours notice, with little correlation between the severity or importance of a power and the notice period.

Warrants

A warrant is an order issued by a JP. It is applied for by a person entitled to use a power of entry, which could variously be a police officer, a local authority inspector, a customs officer or an official of a central government department. Many statutes provide that a warrant may be sought in support of a power of entry, and where one is granted, it allows its recipient to use force to gain access to the premises mentioned in the warrant.

Unlike a "document showing authority", a warrant is a legal document, and means that the exercise of the power in question has been considered and approved by an independent person (ie a magistrate). The official applying for the warrant will have to go before the magistrate and give "information on oath", meaning that they will need to swear on the Bible or other holy book, or make a secular "affirmation", that what they tell the magistrate is true. They will need to "satisfy" the magistrate that the requirements for the issue of a warrant under the legislation establishing the entry power are fulfilled. This usually means that they will need to show a good reason for entering the premises, and sometimes that entry has already been refused or that the premises are empty and the occupier cannot be contacted.

A warrant issued after such an application must at least specify the legislation under which it is granted, the name of the official who is authorised to enter, and the address of the premises to be entered.[13] There is no need for it to carry any reference to the purpose of the entry, or the magistrate's reasons for being "satisfied" that a warrant should be issued.

Some powers specify that the warrant should be shown to the occupier when entry is made to the premises (assuming of course that he or she is present). However, this is an exception rather than a rule and the great majority of powers are silent on the issue.

A small number of powers require supervision and authorisation by a higher judicial authority than a JP. Usually this means a Circuit Judge (a full-time, professional, legally-trained judge used to presiding over a Crown Court or County Court). Powers requiring orders to be issued at this level are typically those involving a search for evidence which could result in the occupier of the premises being charged with a serious offence, an example being the power under the Drug Trafficking Act 1994.

---

13 *R v Inland Revenue Commissioners, ex parte Rossminster* [1980] AC 952.

Where an entry power provides for the issue of a warrant, the warrant can typically be issued only in specified circumstances, reflecting factors which prevent entry without a warrant being a realistic alternative. The following list of requirements for the issue of a warrant comes from Section 32 of the Food Safety Act 1990, and this formula is widespread amongst powers in this category.[14]

(2) If a justice of the peace, on sworn information in writing, is satisfied that there is reasonable ground for entry into any premises for any such purpose as is mentioned in subsection (1) above and either—

(a) that admission to the premises has been refused, or a refusal is apprehended, and that notice of the intention to apply for a warrant has been given to the occupier; or

(b) that an application for admission, or the giving of such a notice, would defeat the object of the entry, or that the case is one of urgency, or that the premises are unoccupied or the occupier temporarily absent,

the justice may by warrant signed by him authorise the authorised officer to enter the premises, if need be by reasonable force.

The above formula does however permit a warrant to be obtained in two situations in which it is arguably unnecessary. Firstly, under subsection (2) (a), forcible entry under a warrant can be effected if "a refusal is apprehended"; in other words if the householder has not refused to allow officials to enter, but the officials believe that he or she may do so. There is no requirement that officials use their best endeavours to ascertain whether consent to the entry will be given or withheld, nor is it required

14 Food Safety Act 1990, Section 2 (2).

that any notice given to the occupier make clear that silence on their part could give rise to an "apprehended refusal".

Secondly, under subsection (2) (b), officials may break into a dwelling under warrant if the occupier is "temporarily absent". There is no guidance on how long a householder would have to be away from their property to count as "temporarily absent" and therefore liable to have their home broken into while they are away. It is quite conceivable that an occupier who had gone on holiday, for example, could return to find that the notice period (typically between 24 hours and 7 days) had expired, and that officials had obtained a warrant, forced entry to the house and carried out a search. Importantly, officials seeking a warrant on grounds of "temporary absence" do not need to show that there would be any disadvantage in delaying the entry until the occupier's return, as issues of urgency or the fear of concealment by a returning occupier are separate, alternative grounds.

Reasonable Time

A majority of entry powers provide that they are to be exercised at "any reasonable hour". There is no guidance in statutory law on what counts as a reasonable hour, and it is left to the official exercising the power to decide. If challenged in court, the court will consider the factual circumstances. Generally speaking, entry to a dwelling will need to be carried out during daylight hours when residents can be expected to be awake, while entry onto business premises may be reasonable at a different time, depending on the industry in question. For example, it may be reasonable to inspect the operations of a casino at midnight, but not to demand entry to a house in order to remove an electricity meter at the same time.

Where private dwellings are concerned, the courts have not laid down a consistent standard. As recently as 2002, the High Court has considered 6am to be a reasonable time for a home to be searched,[15] while at other times entry at 7am has been regarded as unreasonably early.[16]

Where a power is exercised under warrant, these considerations usually do not apply and entry may be effected at any time. This reflects the fact that warrants are often sought in order to seize evidence before it can be concealed or destroyed, so that surprise is of the essence. However, there are many times when this is not the case, and the warrant has been issued because the householder has refused access. Occupiers may have good reason to refuse to allow officials to enter, so it seems unnecessary that they should lose the protection of entry "at a reasonable time" for so doing.

15 *Kent Pharmaceuticals Ltd v Director of the Serious Fraud Office* [2002] EWHC 3023.

16 *R v Inland Revenue Commissioners, ex parte Rossminster* [1980] AC 952.

CHAPTER NINE

A DAY IN THE LIFE OF A BRITISH SUBJECT

POWERS OF ENTRY are not an abstract legal concept in which only constitutional lawyers need take an interest. Most British citizens will come into contact at some time with an official entitled to enter their property. Often this is for a mundane purpose, such as to read the gas or electricity meter. But the 266 laws identified in this paper cover a wide range of real life situations.

The events recounted in the following imaginary chronology are based on real entry powers, presented in the way in which their respective establishing laws allow them to be exercised. Although unlikely, a day such as this could theoretically happen. The chronology illustrates one of the key problems with the current state of entry powers under UK law – while most officials would use them responsibly, many are drafted so broadly that there is little to stop over-zealous or officious personnel using their powers in an unreasonable, oppressive or unnecessary manner.

Imagine that our citizen, John Smith, lives on a farm somewhere in England with his wife Patricia and their three children. They employ two part-time staff to help run the operation. John looks after the running of the farm, while Patricia practises as an accountant from her home office in the farmhouse, acting for a small number of local clients and looking after the money for the farm.

07:15 It is a quiet morning in the Smith household. John and Patricia are drinking tea in bed when Patricia hears a noise from outside. John goes to investigate and sees two men trudging across the small paddock in front of the farmhouse with an odometer.

"What are you two playing at?" enquires John, leaning out of the window.

"Measuring your footpath, mate," replies one of the men, defiantly brandishing a sheet of paper with an official letterhead. John realises they are talking about the dirt track that leads across the corner of the paddock and asks why they need to measure it, to which they reply that they need to see if it is wide enough and in good enough condition to give the public proper access to the property.

"We did warn you two weeks ago, sir," insists the other inspector. Dimly, John remembers getting a letter on the subject, and his concerns are eased slightly.

"Couldn't you have come a bit later?" he enquires. "You gave my wife a shock clattering in here at this time in the morning."

"Got to get on with the job, mate," answers the first workman. "We can start when we like, you know."

Law: Under Section 108 (1) of the National Parks and Access to the Countryside Act 1949, a person authorised in writing by DEFRA may enter land to survey it in connection with the making of an Access Order. 14 days' notice must be given. Obstructing a surveyor carries a fine of £200.

07:54 After getting dressed, John decides to check on the progress of the footpath inspectors. By the time he gets to the front door both men are gone, but his eye is caught by another man in the opposite corner of the field, who appears to be fiddling with the lock on the gate that leads from the road. As John walks over, he can hear him tutting and sees him scribbling on a clipboard.

"Morning, can I help you?" asks John pointedly.

"Yes, perhaps you can explain this," replies the stranger, tapping the padlock with his biro.

"What do you mean explain it? I don't want people getting in here at night. My neighbour had his car nicked the other week and you know what police numbers are round here."

"Hmmmm, no, that won't do sir," scolds the stranger, shaking his head. "This is open country, isn't it?"

"Well, it's my farm actually. I live here, it's my property".

The stranger rummages in his briefcase and pulls out an ordnance survey map. "Look, right here, it's marked as open country. Just because it's yours doesn't mean it's not open country. The public have a right to roam and you, sir, are violating that right with your padlock."

John wonders how the public's right to roam trumps his right to secure his property, but the day's getting on and he can't get into an argument. As he walks off, the access inspector pulls out a camera and snaps several shots of the offending lock before leaving to compile his report.

Law: *Section 40 of the Countryside and Rights of Way Act 2000 allows an officer of an "appropriate countryside body" to enter private land "for the purpose of ascertaining whether members of the public are being permitted to exercise the right [to roam]". He may take a police officer with him, and there is a £500 fine for obstruction. No notice need be given if the occupier has previously been ordered to remove an obstruction.*

08:12 Patricia collects the post from the doormat. Most is correspondence from her clients but there are two letters addressed "to whom it may concern," one from the Natural Environment Research Council and one from the Ordnance Survey. Both say that their surveyors will be visiting the Smiths' farm shortly. Patricia puts the letters to one side, meaning to write back and ask for more information.

08:31 Two vans pull up in the driveway at the front of the house and disgorge five officials, two wearing Ordnance Survey badges and three with the logo of the Natural Environment Research Council. Annoyed, Patricia goes out to remonstrate.

"What are you lot doing?" she asks. "I haven't given permission for this yet."

"We don't need your permission, love," replies an Ordnance Survey official. "It's a power of entry, innit?"

"Well surely you should at least have given me some warning!" insists Patricia.

"We did, we wrote to you. Not our fault if you don't read your post, is it?"

"I did read the post, but it only came 20 minutes ago! I mean what kind of notice is 20 minutes?"

"Ah, but the law doesn't say how long the notice has got to be," grins the surveyor, "just that it has to be written. And it was".

"Oh, very well," says Patricia, surrendering to the inevitable. "But isn't half past eight a little early? Don't you have to do this at a reasonable time or something like that?"

"True, true," the surveyor sniffs defensively. "But it's up to us to decide what's reasonable, there's no hours specified in the law. And since you're up and dressed, it seems pretty reasonable to me."

Law: Section 1 of the Geological Survey Act 1845 permits a person employed by the Natural Environment Research Council, and any persons assisting them, to enter private land. Written notice must be given, but no notice period is specified. The surveyors may "break up the surface" of the land and fix any stone, post or mark. Entry must be at a reasonable time, and there is a £20 fine for obstruction. Section 2 of the Ordnance Survey Act is in almost identical terms, but obstructing anyone acting under this legislation carries a fine of £200.

09:20 John is beginning his day's work on the farm. As he nears the chicken-sheds he hears a squawk and, looking round, sees another suited, clipboard-wielding figure emerge from the nearest chicken-shed.

"Well, that all looks in order," beams the inspector, brushing feathers from his jacket.

"What looks in order?"

"Your poultry. Not being inhumanely slaughtered."

"Well why on earth would they be?" gasps John. "This isn't a poultry farm, we only keep them for their eggs. Anyway, who complained that they were being treated cruelly?"

"Oh, we don't need a complaint, sir. Just reason to believe chickens have been slaughtered here previously. Could just have been a couple."

John suddenly remembers the two fallow hens he had finished off and taken to the farmers' market at the weekend. He is left to contemplate his relief at being cleared as the inspector walks off back to his car.

Law: Under Section 4 (1) of the Slaughter of Poultry Act 1967, an inspector authorised by the local authority or by DEFRA may enter premises where the slaughter of poultry appears to have been in progress within 48 hours of the entry, in order to ascertain whether there has been any breach of any provisions of the Act. Anyone obstructing the inspector can be fined £500.

09:58 Patricia is in her office upstairs in the farmhouse, looking over some papers a client has sent her. One of them is an ex-civil servant at the MoD who has made some money writing an exposé of corruption in arms contracts. Just as Patricia is filling in his tax return, there is a stern rap on the door. Opening it, Patricia is stunned to see two CID officers holding up their warrant cards.

"Open up please Madam," says the first. "Official Secrets Act."

"Official secrets?" says Patricia. "I'm not going to disclose any."

"Maybe you're not, but we think your client is and we're here to get the evidence," insists the officer as he pushes past her into the office.

"Wait a minute," replies Patricia. "I know the law, you need a warrant from a magistrate for this sort of thing. Let's see it."

"No we don't," comes the muffled reply from the office, where the officers are already opening draws and rifling through files. "Our superintendent authorised it without asking a magistrate. It's an emergency you see."

"Who says it's an emergency?" demands Patricia.

The officers glance at one another a little sheepishly. "Erm...the superintendent."

"So you mean he himself gets to decide whether he can override the normal procedure? He doesn't have to get anyone's permission?"

"Nope. Oh well, can't see anything secret here. We'll be off. Mind how you go, ma'am."

Law: Section 9 (2) of the Official Secrets Act 1911 allows a police superintendent to give a written order to a constable authorising him to enter any premises named in the order and to search for and seize any document. The power arises when the superintendent believes that an offence under the Act has been or is about to be committed, and that the case is one of "great emergency". The superintendent's belief does not have to be reasonable.

10:19 Having finished his work in the chicken yard, John is now on his way to do some chores in one of the storage sheds. As he nears it, the sound of crashing and clanking from within alerts him that all is not as it should be. Entering, he spies two officials rummaging through the storage cabinets, examining the floor, and sniffing the contents of cans and containers.

"What the blazes are you two looking for?" asks John, slightly impatient at the continued disturbance to his morning.

"Milk," replies the first inspector.

"Yes. Hidden, illicit milk," confirms the second, eyeballing John. "You wouldn't know anything about that now, would you sir?"

"What? No, of course I wouldn't. Why on earth would I have illicit milk?"

"Didn't you used to have a milking herd here, sir?"

John scratches his head. "That was a couple of years ago, we had a dozen or so. But we gave up dairy because it just wasn't making a profit what with the prices the way they are."

"Aha! So you *did* have milk here! Do you still?"

"No, I just told you. Anyway what if I did, what business is it of yours?"

"You get compensation for producers exiting the milk market. Just checking you're not ripping us off, that's all."

"Ripping you off? You really think I'd go to the trouble of having secret cows?"

"You never know. It has happened."

"Really? Where? Where have you found camouflaged cows, for goodness' sake?"

"Can't discuss operational matters, sir. Anyway, this place checks out. Thank you for your time."

Law: Under Section 2 of the Milk (Cessation of Production) Act 1985, an authorised officer of DEFRA may enter any land occupied by any person who has received a payment in compensation for having reduced or ceased milk production, in order to determine whether that person is still engaged in milk production. The inspector may require the occupier to provide him with any records or accounts, and may take them away with him. There is a £5,000 fine for obstructing the inspector.

10:47 Back in the office, Patricia is clearing up the mess the police officers left when there is a ring at the doorbell. This time it's a woman from the Department of Work and Pensions.

"Are you Patricia Smith?" asks the woman.

"Yes, how can I help you?"

"You employ people here, don't you?"

"Well, if you mean the two labourers we have part time, then yes. It's all above board and on the books, they get National Insurance and everything."

"Ah, but do they get the minimum wage?"

"Yes. Well, more than the minimum actually; they're good workers. Who says different?"

"Nobody says different, but I get to check anyway. Stand aside please."

The DWP Inspector spends 20 minutes leafing through Patricia's accounts, checking the payments made to the Smiths' two staff. Patricia is getting a little impatient. "Look," she says, "I've already lost most of my morning, I need to get on with my work. Could you hurry up, please?"

"I wouldn't obstruct me if I were you, madam. There's a £5,000 fine for that." Patricia backs off and leaves the inspector to get on with it.

Law: Section 14 of the National Minimum Wage Act 1998 allows an inspector to enter any premises used in connection with the business of "a person who supplies work to an individual who qualifies for the national minimum wage", in order to require the production of documents. There is a £5,000 fine for obstructing the inspector.

11:30 Still shaking his head in disbelief at the milk inspectors, John is making his way back to the farmhouse for a quick cup of coffee when his eye is caught by a tall man in a trench coat striding across the east field towards the boundary of the property.

"Hey!" John calls after him. "Who are you?"

The man stops and waits for John to catch up with him. Then he pulls out a warrant card. "Her Majesty's Revenue and Customs, sir. Investigating duty evasion."

"Duty evasion? What am I supposed to have done now?"

The officer puts a comforting hand on John's shoulder. "It's nothing to do with you, sir. It's the little brewery next door. They've got a pipeline and I'm off to check it. I'm just passing through."

"Oh," breathes John, rather relieved. "Well, I don't mind that. But you could at least have asked or something."

"Well I don't need to ask, do I? I've got a power."

"It would have been polite, that's all."

"Yep, well, there's no code of conduct. I don't have to be polite. Move along now please sir." With that he strides off towards the boundary.

Law: Section 162 of the Customs and Excise Management Act 1979 provides a Customs officer with a power to enter any land adjacent to a pipeline through which a dutiable substance flows.

11:59 The farmhouse doorbell rings again, and this time Patricia is surprised to see an inspector from OFSTED, the schools inspectorate. The inspector asks for Charlotte Smith, John and Patricia's eldest daughter. Charlotte, 20, is an aspiring actress, but when work is slow she stays at her parents' house and makes a little money by looking after the children of busy neighbours during the day. The farmhouse has a large garden and a playroom that Charlotte and her brothers have grown out of. All the children and their parents have been delighted by the service and have never complained about any aspect of it. Charlotte comes to the door to find out what OFSTED want with her.

"Charlotte Smith?"

"Yes, what can I do for you?"
"Are you providing childcare here?"
"Well, yes, I'm looking after three of the neighbours' kids today. They're playing in the garden. Why?"
"And do you do this for reward?"
"Their parents each give me £20 when they pick them up, if that's what you mean. I'd hardly call it a business."
"Doesn't matter," replies the OFSTED man sternly. "You need to be registered, and you're not. Now I'd like to come and see what's happening please."
"Registered?" queries a puzzled Charlotte, "what for? I only do this for a few family friends, and they all know me."
"Doesn't matter. Now let me see those children." Charlotte leads him into the garden where the neighbours' children are playing happily. The Inspector is satisfied and leaves after being squirted with a water pistol and made to go in goal.
"Right, well they'll serve an Enforcement Notice on you next week, I should imagine," he advises Charlotte as he packs up his things. "I can see there's no problem here, but you still have to be registered. I'll come back and check again next month."

Law: Under Section 77 (1) of the Childcare Act 2006, an inspector authorised by the Chief Inspector of Schools may enter any premises in England where he has reason to believe that early years childminding is taking place without a licence. A police officer may assist, and there is a £2,500 fine for obstruction.

12:28 Back on the working part of the farm, John has been uninterrupted for over 40 minutes and is starting to believe he might be able to finish one or two of the tasks he had planned for the day. As he walks towards the garage where he keeps his mower, he hears a rustling of branches. Turning towards the sound, John spies a pair of hands and a pair of smartly-shod feet wrapped round the trunk of the old oak tree in the corner of the meadow. With a thud, a stocky, middle-aged man drops down out of the tree, dusts himself down and scribbles in a notebook.

"I hope you're not on your way to prune this tree," hails the stranger as John walks over to him.

"What if I am? It's my tree," replies John. He had no intention of pruning it but doesn't like being told what he can and can't do on his own property.

"It needs work doing to it. Not safe, that isn't. Could fall and harm persons or property. You wait, there'll be a notice in the post telling you what you need to do to it to make it safe."

"It doesn't look unsafe to me," insists John, "but I'll have my pal Ben come and take a look at it. He's a tree surgeon."

The inspector sucks his teeth disapprovingly. "I'm afraid what we say goes, sir. We're the local authority, and if we say it needs work done, then it gets done."

"Well, thanks for your advice, I'll bear it in mind," says John, deciding to stick up for himself. "But seeing as this is my tree and on my land, I'll do what I like with it."

"Suit yourself, sir," shrugs the inspector, snapping his notepad shut. "But if it's not done in a few weeks, I'm afraid we'll have to send a council team over here, do the work ourselves, and then invoice you for their time and trouble. Much better to do it yourself, sir."

"I won't let them in, then!" John calls after him.

"They'll come in anyway," the inspector shouts back as he leaves, "even if they have to do it at two in the morning. They can do that, you know."

Law: Section 24 of the Local Government (Miscellaneous Provisions) Act 1976 allows an officer of a local authority to enter land in order to decide whether any action should be taken in respect of any tree on the land. It also permits council officers to enter the land in order to carry out work on a tree under Section 23. In either case, entry does not have to be at a reasonable time.

13:05 Patricia has finished putting her papers back together and is about to make some lunch for herself and the rest of the family, but is interrupted by another ring at the doorbell.

"What can I do for you?" Patricia asks the short, business-suited man on the doorstep.

"Child Support Agency, madam," replies the man curtly as he reaches into his pocket and pulls out a document. "I have an authorisation here from the Secretary of State. Where's Edward Jenkins?"

"Edward Jen...oh, you mean Ted, our labourer?"

"Where is he?"

"He's not at work today, he's only part time. Why, what's he done?"

"We're checking up on his maintenance payments to his ex-wife. I'll need to come inside."

"Oh, I see," says Patricia, standing aside to let the inspector pass. "But we deduct those for him automatically, you must have been getting them."

"Yes, we have. Just want to check he's not earning more than you say he is."

"But that's silly," protests Patricia. "There was a woman from the DWP here this morning. She checked how much both of our workers are paid. Why can't you just ask her?"

"Different department," the inspector answers as he starts rummaging through the office. "We need to see for ourselves."

Law: Section 14 of the Child Support Act 1991 allows an inspector authorised by the Secretary of State to enter any premises "which are used by any specified person for the purpose of carrying on any trade, profession, vocation or business". The inspector may question anyone over the age of 18 on the premises, and any occupier of the premises is legally obliged to "furnish to the inspector all such information and documents as the inspector may reasonably require". Any person who obstructs the inspector, or who "refuses or neglects to answer any question or furnish any information or to produce any document when required to do so", can be fined £1,000.

13:11 "So much for joined-up government!" thinks Patricia as she reaches the kitchen, having left the CSA man to get on with his investigations. Just then something catches her eye through the window.

"John, look!" she calls to her husband as he walks in. "Out there! What's that chap doing taking photographs of our trees?"

"Oh, not that clown again," sighs John, "I've only just been talking to him. I'll go and see what he wants now.

"What are you playing at?" he calls to the photographer as he approaches. "I only just spoke to your lot. I told you, I'll have a think about that work you said needs doing, but you've got to give me a chance!"

"Eh?" asks the photographer, looking puzzled.

"Aren't you from the council – you know, for the 'dangerous tree' work?"

"Nah, not me mate. Forestry Commission." The photographer points to the logo on his breast pocket. "Just here to inspect your timber stock. Part of our cataloguing work."

"Well, who says you can…"

"This does." The photographer pulls out an official Forestry Commission order. "Now you'd better let me get on with it, or you'll be fined £1,000."

Law: Under Section 48 of the Forestry Act 1967, an officer of the Forestry Commission may "enter and survey any land [...] for the purpose of inspecting any timber thereon". The inspector does not have to give notice, but must show his authority if asked. There is a £1,000 fine for obstruction.

14:02 David Smith, John and Patricia's eldest son, is at the stable where the family keep their 10-year-old pony, Fred. David, 18, will be going to university in the autumn, and has been using his summer holiday to build up some savings by giving riding lessons. A pupil is coming at 3pm, so David has arrived to muck out, groom and tack up Fred in advance.

"Here you go boy!" calls David, holding out a handful of Polo mints into the stable. He is surprised when, instead of Fred's chestnut brown nose, out pops a smiling, bespectacled head wearing a flat cap.

"Thanks!" says the stranger, taking a Polo. "I think I'm done here."

"What?" asks a still stunned David. "Who on earth are you?"

"I'm from the council. Riding Establishments Inspectorate."

"Riding Establishments? But we've only got one pony, I had him when I was a kid. He's just a pet."

"You give riding lessons here though, don't you?"

"Well, just a few, to friends' children mostly."

"Then that makes this a Riding Establishment, young sir. And it's my job to inspect them. Doesn't matter if you've only got one pony. Anyway, all looks in order so I'm off to write my report for the council." With that the inspector strolls away, leaving David and Fred to wonder who had tipped him off.

Law: Section 6 of the Riding Establishments Act 1964 defines a "riding establishment" as any premises where horses are kept for "the purpose of their being used in providing, in return for payment, instruction in riding". Section 2 of the same Act gives an authorised officer of a local authority power to enter, at any reasonable time, "any premises where they have reason to believe a person is keeping a riding establishment", in order to inspect them. No notice need be given, and any person obstructing the inspector can be fined £500.

14:40 John is lifting a heavy bag of fertiliser onto his trailer. As he wipes his brow, he hears a shrill voice calling after him. "Hey! You! Stop right there!" Turning, John sees two men sprinting towards him, one carrying a large briefcase.

"Don't touch that fertiliser!" shouts the first one. John stands back and watches as they reach the trailer, grab the topmost bag and pull it down onto the ground with a loud thud. One man cuts open the bag, while the other spoons samples of fertiliser into plastic containers he has pulled out of his briefcase.

"What's all this in aid of then?" asks a bewildered John. "I need that for my cabbage field!"

"Fertiliser inspections, sir," replies the first official. "Got to make sure it all complies with the relevant directives. Can't have you spreading the wrong stuff on your land."

"I understand that," replies John, "but I bought this stuff from the wholesaler, I don't produce it."

"Yeah, but you're storing it."

"You're talking about the dozen bags in my shed?"

"Hmmm, well it looked more like 15 or 20 to me, sir. Anyway, doesn't matter how much of it you have, if you're storing it we get to come and check it." The second man snaps his briefcase shut and the pair head off back to the lab with their samples.

Law: Section 76 of the Agriculture Act 1970 allows an inspector to enter any premises where he has reason to believe that fertiliser purchased by the occupier of the premises is kept. He may take with him any other persons and any equipment he believes necessary, and may take samples of any fertiliser found there. Obstructing the inspector carries a fine of £1,000.

15:12 Patricia is trying to get down to work, but is distracted by a voice from outside, slowly counting. "…four, five. Six. Seven, eight." Intrigued as well as annoyed, Patricia makes her way to the paddock in front of the farmhouse. There she sees a young man in an anorak and boots, shielding his eyes with one hand and pointing at different spots in the meadow with the other while counting out loud."

Patricia coughs politely. "Mind if I ask what you're doing there?"

"Counting your rabbits, ma'am," explains the inspector. "Except the rotten little things will keep hopping around, so it's hard. I'm sure I've counted that one over there twice. Anyway, it's for pest control. Very important."

"You don't need to tell me it's important, we're running a farm!" replies Patricia. "But why didn't you just ask first? I'd have had my husband send you an estimate. He knows this land better than anyone."

"Oh. Didn't think of that." The man looks taken aback. "The law just says we can come on and inspect, there's nothing in there about asking first. I've got an authorisation from DEFRA, you know."

Law: Section 1 of the Pests Act 1954 gives a DEFRA officer the power to enter any land at a reasonable time, in order to inspect it for the purposes of determining whether it should be designated as a "rabbit clearance area".

15:49 David and his young pupil are on the way back from their riding lesson, with Fred having recovered from the shock of having a stranger in his stable. The bridleway through the nearby woods leads across part of the Smiths' land, although few local riders use it. As David, Fred and their pupil make their way back to the stable, they come across a man in a shirt and tie blocking their way. He doesn't notice them at first as he is busy stamping his foot on the path, prodding it with his pen and scraping at it with a ruler. Fred's confused whinny catches his attention.

"Afternoon, young man. You from this farm?" the man enquires.

"Yes, it's my parents'," David responds, "and this is their private property. What are you doing on it?"

"Checking this bridleway, and it's a good thing I did," the inspector scolds. "The surface is all broken up. Why, a horse could... could... well, I don't know really but it's not right anyway. You're going to have to resurface this, or we'll do it ourselves and your dad will have to pay for it."

"I think it'll be mum who pays for it actually, but..."

"Well anyway, just make sure it gets done. I'll be back in a few weeks to check up on it."

Law: Under Section 7 of the Rights of Way Act 1990, an inspector authorised by a local authority may enter land for any purpose connected with the authority's power to make good the surface of a footpath or bridleway. No notice need be given if the entry is carried out in order to gather information. Section 9 of the Act allows the authority to recoup the cost of the works from the occupier of the land.

16:30 Having finished laying fertiliser on his cabbages, John is heaving the remaining bags and his tools back into the main storage shed. It's dark inside, so he pulls the string that powers the strip light fixed to the ceiling.

"Ha! Just as I thought!" cries a voice from the dim recesses of the shed. Out steps a woman with a clipboard under her arm and a beeping light-meter in the other. "Far, far too dark. One of your staff could come in here, tread on that rake, stun himself, trip over the lawnmower and fall into the shredder. Then you'd really be for it."

"Oh, and how many times has that happened exactly?" queries an increasingly irritated John.

"Erm, never; but only because of the vigilance of all of us at the Health and Safety Executive! I'd clean up your act if I were you, sir, and think about installing some proper lighting, a first aid kid, a panic button and a warning sign translated into all the languages spoken by your workforce. We'll be sending you our observations." With that she stalks off, leaving John trying hard to remember the last time there'd been any sort of accident on the farm.

Law: *Under Section 20 of the Health and Safety at Work Act 1974, an inspector of the Health and Safety Executive or the local authority may enter any premises which he has reason to believe it is necessary for him to enter for a purpose for which he has been appointed. Entry must normally be at a reasonable time, but the inspector may enter at any time if he believes the situation to be dangerous. This belief does not have to be reasonable. The inspector can take a police officer with him, and any equipment he believes necessary. Once on the premises the inspector has wide powers to take samples, remove objects, or close down parts of the premises, and to question any person present and require them to give a signed statement. There is a £5,000 fine for obstructing the inspector.*

17:16 Patricia has finished her work for the day and is calming down with a cup of tea when the doorbell rings once more. Wearily, Patricia gets up and answers the door.

"I'd like to see your plate, please," announces the well-built man standing in the porch, "and I've got a warrant here to search for it." He flourishes a signed document.

"My plate? Which one?"

"I think you know which one, madam. The knocked-off one, that's what."

"Knocked off? What on earth are you talking about?"

The man hands her the warrant, which identifies him as a representative of the Receiver of Wreck, and shoves past her into the living room.

"Aha! This is the one," he announces, grabbing an old decorative platter from the mantelpiece.

"What? Get your hands off that! We found that on the beach during our holiday, it's perfectly legitimate."

"Well, I have reason to believe that this came from a shipwreck. And that means it's mine. Let that be a lesson to you." With that he wraps the platter in bubble-wrap and leaves with it under his arm.

Law: Section 247 of the Merchant Shipping Act 1995 allows an officer authorised by the Receiver of Wreck to enter any premises where an item from a shipwreck is "in the possession of some person who is not the owner of it" and to "search for, seize and detain" any such item.

19:28 The family are gathered in the living room after dinner, discussing their disrupted day.

"I've got very little done today," complains Patricia, "and I'm behind with my clients."

"Same here, love," says John. "Every way I turn there's been some busybody on my case. It's amazing."

"And poor old Fred's never seen so many people in his life," chuckles David.

"Never mind," puts in Charlotte, "let's watch that TV show that comes on at half past. That always cheers us up."

As the family turn to watch the TV, the French windows open and in struts an official, clipboard in hand, pointing accusingly at the set.

"I hope you've got a licence for that!"

Law: Section 366 of the Communications Act 2003 provides for a JP to issue a warrant allowing an OFCOM inspector, along with any number of police officers, to enter any premises or vehicle at any time, using reasonable force, in order to search for evidence of unlicensed TV watching. Any person who obstructs an OFCOM official exercising this power can be fined £5,000.

CHAPTER TEN

THE CASE FOR A REFORM BILL

TO PROVIDE A SINGLE, over-arching entry power for government officials would greatly simplify the current system and harmonise its procedural requirements. However, it would do so at a cost of effectively sacrificing English law's admirable tradition of restraining the executive's powers within the bounds of necessity.

There is however an alternative course which could succeed in providing the citizen with a clear, concrete and consistent set of rules on who can enter his property, while still preserving the principle that the state enjoys no such power without Parliament's specific and limited authorisation. This solution would take the form of an Act of Parliament providing a common form for existing and future powers, but not assigning those powers to any person or organisation. Specific legislation would continue to be the source of entry powers – both those catalogued in the Appendix to this paper and any passed in the future – while the new Act would set out how those powers are to be exercised and how they are monitored and recorded.

When enacted, the new legislation could be accompanied by a Schedule setting out all the currently existing entry powers whose form and procedure is to be replaced by that set out in the Act. Future legislation establishing entry powers would refer to this Act when creating a new power, rather than setting out separate terms. For example, a new power of entry in a future Bill under this system might provide that:

A person authorised in writing by the Secretary of State shall, for the purposes of discharging his responsibilities under this Act, be entitled to exercise a power of entry in the form specified by Section 4 of the Entry Powers Act 2007.

This would mean that a citizen need only read a single piece of legislation – the proposed Entry Powers Act – in order to be familiar with the procedure under which his home may be entered and his rights to object to that entry. However, it would continue to be the case that there was no single, general power; so that the state could only enter private dwellings in circumstances specifically contemplated and approved by Parliament.

An Entry Powers Act would also provide an opportunity for more general reform. Thus, the problems of unnecessarily broad drafting identified throughout this paper could be remedied and new procedural forms implemented to create a more satisfactory balance between the needs of the state and the rights of the citizen. This chapter suggests a number of principles that should underpin the single, consistent procedure enshrined in an Entry Powers Act.

Permission should always be sought where possible

An entry power is, in essence, a right to go onto an occupier's premises without his permission. There are many public officials who regularly enter citizen's homes as guests invited or at least permitted by the occupier – health visitors, social workers, special needs education officers and the like. Such people are not exercising a power of entry, they come into the home on the basis of a licence (the explicit or implied consent of the occupier).

The fact that a particular class of official is entitled to exercise a power of entry does not of course prevent them from nevertheless seeking permission to come onto the premises. To do so is not only polite, it is democratic: if permission is gained then entry is effected without an actual entry power having been invoked, and an instance of the state's exercise of power over the individual has been avoided. To ask permission should in any case br best practice from a practical point of view.

While the laws establishing powers of entry frequently require that notice be given to the occupier of the premises, this is not the same as a request for permission. The tenor of the interaction between citizen and state is very different when the occupier is *asked* to when he is merely *informed*.

There is therefore a strong argument for replacing the concept of "notice" with that of asking permission. A document asking permission would have to include all the same details normally required in a notice – the date and time at which entry is proposed, its purpose, and the number of people who will be carrying it out – but would explicitly ask for the householder's consent to the entry. Only if this was withheld would the matter be put on the footing of an "entry power".

Without permission, there must be a warrant

Naturally, there are occasions when the requirement for an element of surprise means that asking permission would be self-defeating. When entry powers are exercised in order to seek evidence of the citizen's misconduct, the law typically provides that a JP's warrant should be obtained and entry effected without notice; provided that the magistrate is satisfied by information on oath that this is necessary. The same system would of course apply if "notice" were replaced with "request".

A new Entry Powers Act would provide that, where permission is refused (or will not be sought, because of the need for surprise), then a JP's warrant should always be obtained, with exceptions only for saving life and limb and for arrests carried out under the Police and Criminal Evidence Act. Implementation of such a principle would bring the UK into line with most of the developed common law world by abolishing the Writ of Assistance. It would also resolve the lacuna in the drafting of the Category Three powers, whereby non-consensual entry can be effected without a warrant so long as no force is used.

Finally, such a reform would solve the problem of the Category Four powers, which have been drafted in such a way that no warrant is available but which the courts have interpreted as authorising the use of force. Under a new Act, Category Four would vanish altogether and these powers would join Category Three, to be exercised only with permission or with a warrant.

Warrant applications should be a form of scrutiny

When an officer seeking to exercise a power of entry under the new Act without the permission of the occupier, he should need to apply to a JP for a warrant. Such an application should be an opportunity for the magistrate – and, where possible, the occupier of the premises to be entered – to examine the official's case and conduct and come to a decision about whether the entry is necessary. To an extent this is already the case, but the law could be more specific in providing for particular enquiries to be made. A future Act should specify that a JP must enquire:

- whether permission has been sought for the entry to take place, and whether the occupier is or ought reasonably to be aware that it has been sought.
- if permission has not been sought in order to prevent the occupier becoming aware of the intended entry, is there sufficient evidence for the JP to satisfy himself that this is necessary and proportionate?
- if permission has not been sought because the occupier is away, is the requirement for entry of sufficient urgency that it should be effected before the occupier returns?
- if permission was sought but refused, why was this the case? Were the officials rude? Did they fail to explain what they wanted to do and why? Did the householder refuse outright,

or merely insist that the entry should be at a different time, or with fewer people?

In cases where a warrant is sought because entry is refused, the occupier should be given notice that an application for a warrant is to be made. He should be given an opportunity to be present at the hearing, to hear the official's case and to put his own points to the magistrate.

Warrants should be evidence – for the benefit of the occupier and the wider public – that the exercise of an entry power has been independently scrutinised and authorised. The document itself should therefore always specify who had applied for the warrant and under what law, when the application was heard and by whom, and on what grounds the determination had been made in the applicant's favour.

A "reasonable time" should be specified

The principle that an entry power be exercised at a reasonable time is firmly established in the current law, despite the fact that the widespread inconsistency identified above means it is not always referred to in individual Acts. Where the law is silent on the issue, the courts have held that there is no limit to the range of times at which the beneficiary of the power might choose to enter.[17]

Having public officials choose a reasonable time to act is important both in showing simple courtesy for the citizen, and in giving him a fair opportunity to be awake, aware and ready when his property is entered so that he can supervise the activities of the officials and make any complaints that may be necessary. For the state's servants to choose to enter in the middle of the night is a contributing factor to a power imbalance between them and the citizen: while they are prepared and focused, he is caught off his guard at a time when he is not ready to monitor events.

---

17 *R v Adams* [1980] 1 All ER 473.

As with issues of permission, entry at a reasonable time is not appropriate when it is necessary to avoid giving warning, but it should be a matter of course whenever it is not reasonably believed that evidence may be concealed or destroyed or the investigation obstructed.

Even if the term "at a reasonable time" were to be applied consistently across the range of entry powers, its vagueness allows for the subjective – and surely not neutral – views of the officer effecting the entry to determine the extent of the restriction on his behaviour. The lack of a clear guideline means that one officer might consider entry to a family home at 10pm to be reasonable, while another would hesitate to call after 5pm. Nor have the courts been forthcoming in laying down a firm standard for what constitutes a reasonable time, instead leaving the issue to be determined as one of fact in the individual circumstances.[18]

Naturally where certain commercial activities are concerned, there may be good reasons why inspections should be carried out at night because that is the time of the enterprise's principal business. But where domestic premises are concerned, an Entry Powers Act should lay down a clear standard, specifying that all entry powers should be exercised at a reasonable time, and a time is not reasonable in relation to domestic premises unless it is between the hours of 7am and 9pm.

With the exception of firefighting and similar emergency powers, entry outside these times would be possible only when specified in the warrant, and the JP would have to satisfy himself of the necessity of this derogation before including it.

Proper records should be kept

Powers of entry, no matter how justified, are an infringement against a citizen's right to privacy. Accountability is therefore essential. And there can be no accountability without transparency.

---

[18] *Small v Bickley* (1875) 40 JP 119.

A new Entry Powers Act should specify that every use of an entry power without the permission of the occupier of the premises be recorded. Given that the proposed new regulatory regime would always require a warrant for non-consensual entry, this burden would be minimal and its discharge simple. All that would be needed would be for the JP to keep a copy of the warrant.

Warrants could be automatically collated in a central database. It would then be a simple matter for statistics to be extracted from this database. Proper record-keeping in this manner would be simple and cost-effective, and would enable citizens to obtain information on how many powers were being exercised, which agencies or local authorities were the heaviest and lightest users of them, and how many times they had failed to convince a JP that this use was necessary.

An independent and trusted agency such as the National Audit Office should be given responsibility for collating these statistics and publishing them on an annual basis. Transparency and comparative figures would put pressure on central and local government to use entry powers in a restrained, reasonable and proportionate manner.

CHAPTER ELEVEN

CONCLUSION

THE LAW OF ENTRY as it currently stands is failing citizens. It fails to protect them from over-zealous officials, it fails to provide them with simple and consistent rules on when someone can enter their home, and it fails to ensure that such incidents are properly recorded. In short, it is failing to properly respect their homes.

Every power of entry is in essence a disruption of a citizen's right to privacy in his or her home in favour of the interests of the State. Both legally and in principle, it is an exception to the normal boundaries of the relationship between the private and public realms. The presumption ought to be that these boundaries will be respected, and that they will be set aside only when the wider community – acting through the state – has a legitimate and overriding interest in so doing.

Such a power can be a necessary and proportionate tool for the discharge of the state's duties to its citizens. Today, those duties have multiplied. Government now provides healthcare, social security, education, housing, environmental protection and the enforcement of common standards in numerous fields of private business. The powers catalogued in the Appendix to this paper exist in order to assist the state in meeting these expectations by providing it with the tools to detect and correct infringements of the standards it is charged with upholding.

However, the current legal framework is deficient because its piecemeal, erratic provision of entry powers lets the citizen down, leaving them unsure who can enter their homes and why, at what time, with what level of force, and with what if any independent supervision. The power of the state has expanded at the expense of the freedom of the individual.

A single Act of Parliament to regulate the exercise of entry powers could contribute to remedying these problems by putting all powers on a single footing. It would ensure that the protection already present in the best-drafted laws would be universally applicable. And it would reflect the nation's best and most hallowed legal traditions by enshrining due respect for its citizens' homes. With 266 powers in force and more contemplated, it is high time for Parliament to put its own house in order – and give its citizens security in theirs.

LIST OF ENTRY POWERS EXERCISABLE OVER DOMESTIC PREMISES

1. Manner of listing primary legislation

"Primary legislation" is a term denoting Acts of Parliament. An Act may establish a single entry power (often to carry out the "general functions" of a particular public body), or more commonly specify a number of distinct powers to be used in different circumstances. For example, the Housing Act 1985 provides one entry power to be used in measuring rooms to monitor overcrowding, and a separate entry power to cleanse premises of vermin prior to demolition. While the entry onto premises in either case might well be effected by the same official, the authority under which he steps across the threshold has its source in a different Section of the Housing Act.

It is not always straightforward to distinguish between situations where an Act establishes separate powers, and one where a single power can be used to accomplish a number of objectives. For example an officer of an electricity supplier has a power under the Electricity Act 1989 to "enter during the course of supply", a power that can be used for a wide variety of different functions such as removing a meter, installing a meter, or inspecting the supplier's electrical equipment. In this situation the power can be used for multiple purposes, but derives from a single source within the Electricity Act.

In general, powers within a single Act have been listed as distinct from one another when their procedural requirements or subject matter are different; or when they are established by different Sections of the Act. Sometimes however, powers that are technically distinct are so intimately linked in subject matter, aim and procedure that it would be misleading to list them as separate. Thus, the powers under the Conservation of Seals Act 1970 to inspect a seal population and to carry out a cull following inspection are listed as a single power. This is necessarily a subjective decision, made to ensure that the lists reflect the true range of entry powers and are not skewed by the particular way in which an Act is drafted, whether tending to a single wide-ranging power or multiple similar powers for use in different circumstances.

It is a common occurrence for an Act of Parliament to amend, repeal or supplement a pre-existing piece of legislation. An Act might add entry powers to a previous Act of Parliament, or simply modify the form in which they are exercised. An inspector exercising a power inserted by a new Act of Parliament is technically acting under the old Act, even if that Act did not originally contain such a power. For example, the Care Standards Act 2000 added an entry power into the Children Act 1989 for the inspection of premises where childcare is being provided. Anyone carrying out such an inspection today would count as acting under the Children Act, not under the Care Standards Act. While legally correct, this means of reckoning the source of an entry power can be misleading when discerning trends in the conferment of such powers over time. Listing the power to enter childcare premises under the Children Act 1989 – alongside the other, original powers contained in that Act – would create the impression that the power to carry out such inspections had existed since 1989, when in fact it was created in 2000. Therefore, in situations such as that presented by the Care Standards Act when new powers are inserted into old legislation, they are listed under the title of the Act that effected the insertion, with a note indicating which pre-existing Act was so amended. This listing policy provides a more accurate picture of the dates on which particular powers were first introduced into the law. Where later Acts have not inserted new powers but merely made amendments to the procedure for exercising pre-existing powers, the later, amending Acts are not listed but the amendment is noted under the older Act. This avoids any double-listing of powers.

2. Manner of listing secondary legislation

"Secondary Legislation" is a term used to denote rules, regulations and directives issued by the Government. Many Acts of Parliament provide that Ministers or the Queen in Council may issue such regulations specifying how and when certain provisions of the Act are to be implemented.

Often, Acts of Parliament which establish powers of entry allow a Minister to make regulations governing the circumstances of their use. Such regulations are therefore not a distinct power of entry, but an "incarnation" of one provided by the parent Act of Parliament. Secondary legislation which merely reflects Powers of Entry already present in primary legislation is not included in this Appendix, since to do so would give an inaccurate impression of the number of powers in force.

However, there are two Acts of Parliament which do not specifically create entry powers, but which provide such wide scope for delegated legislation that regulations and orders issued under them have done so. The European Communities Act 1972 allows Ministers to make Regulations in order to give effect to European Union directives in English law, while the United Nations Act gives a similar power to the Queen in Council in respect of decisions of the UN General Assembly.

Secondary legislation under these Acts has been included in the Appendix where it has caused the introduction into English law of a new entry power.

3. Exclusion of powers not permitting entry to dwellings

Legislation which grants powers of entry will specify the types of areas, land or premises, against which the power can be enforced. If a public official is to enter a particular type of land or premises in the purported exercise of a power, that power must be phrased to as to include that type of "target". Whether or not an official can enter private land or a private dwelling house will therefore depend on whether or not the right to do so is granted – explicitly or implicitly – by the legislation authorising entry.

Many entry powers, especially those relating to law enforcement, customs, critical infrastructure such as water and gas, or fire hazards, specify that an inspector can enter "any premises". This broad phrase includes private dwelling houses, and sometimes particular notice requirements or other restrictions are prescribed in relation to the exercise of the power against a person's home. These powers are listed.

Other powers allow entry to "any premises, except those used as a private dwelling"; or specify that for the purposes of that particular Act, the term "premises" does not cover a dwelling. In such cases it is clear that a dwelling cannot be entered. Such powers will only be listed if it is evident from the wording of the statute that entry can still be made to private occupied land, and only structures built on the land are off-limits. In such cases, the restriction against entering a house itself is noted.

The final category of powers are those where the wording shows that a dwelling can be entered provided it has some additional use, usually as a place of business. The form of words used is typically that a person exercising the power may enter any premises "except for premises used only as a dwelling". A house where a business is carried on – perhaps childcare, agriculture or small-scale retail – could be entered. These powers are usually listed, with a note indicating the restriction against entering dwellings that have no business use. However, some powers which are drafted widely enough to encompass such "dual use" premises are not included because of the small likelihood of any such premises existing. Acts which would enable inspections of a private dwelling only so long as it was used as an aerodrome or an oil terminal are excluded.

ENTRY POWERS TABLES

Note on methodology

The principal primary sources used in the original research for the preparation of these Tables were electronic legal databases. These were used to search the text of Acts of Parliament and statutory instruments for terms commonly used when powers of entry are established, and then to confirm that those identified were already in force or awaiting commencement.

A number of secondary sources were also consulted, including *Halsbury's Laws* and *The Law of Entry, Search and Seizure* by Professor Richard Stone.

The information presented in these Tables should be taken as correct on 31 March 2007.

TABLE ONE

POWERS EXPLICITLY ALLOWING THE IMMEDIATE USE OF FORCE WITHOUT A WARRANT

Act Title	Year	Purpose	Form/Requirements
Customs and Excise Management Act	1979	Powers of customs officers to inspect for goods	Can get JP's warrant to search premises. Persons with a Writ of Assistance (customs officer's commission) may enter to search for and seize any goods liable to forfeiture to HMRC, if they are likely to be removed, destroyed or lost before a warrant can be issued. Restriction inserted by Finance Act 2000.
Electricity Act	1989	Entry on premises during course of supply or on discontinuance to inspect equipment, remove meter, install meter etc	Authorised officer of electricity distributor may enter any premises to which electricity supplied. Must give 2 working days' notice for removal of meter. Can get JP's warrant to use reasonable force. Can enter immediately in emergency.
Electricity Act	1989	Repair, replace or alter lines or plant	Must show documentary authority and enter at reasonable time. Five working days' notice required. Can get JP's warrant authorising reasonable force. Can enter immediately without warrant in case of emergency.
Environment Act	1995	Umbrella power for inspection and carrying out of works by Environment Agency and related bodies where danger of serious pollution or damage to health	Must give seven days' notice to enter dwelling. If entry refused, can get warrant to authorise force. In emergency, can effect forcible entry without warrant. Obstruction: £5,000 fine and/or 2 years' prison
Fire Services Act	1947	Fight fire	Immediate right to use force for the purposes of firefighting. Obstruction: £1,000 fine
Intelligence Services Act	1994	Intelligence services entering for purposes of national security	Secretary of State can authorise entry
Landmines Act	1998	Carry out fact-finding mission in accordance with Ottawa Convention on Landmines	If fact-finding mission proposed, Secretary of State may authorise entry. Can get constable to assist, can use reasonable force. Validity of authorisation cannot be questioned in court before mission completed. Obstruction: £5,000 fine

POWERS EXPLICITLY ALLOWING THE IMMEDIATE USE OF FORCE WITHOUT A WARRANT

Act Title	Year	Purpose	Form/Requirements
Police and Criminal Evidence Act	1984	Save life and limb or prevent serious damage to property	Constable may enter with reasonable force at any time. No need for reasonable belief, but this must be his/her purpose.
Police and Criminal Evidence Act	1984	Entry to effect arrest	Constable may enter to arrest for a number of specified offences, for an arrestable offence, or detain someone unlawfully at large whom he has been pursuing.
Police and Criminal Evidence Act	1984	Search premises controlled or occupied by person arrested for an arrestable offence.	Police officer of rank of Inspector or above may authorise officers to enter and search, using reasonable force if necessary, for evidence connected to the offence for which the person was arrested, or a similar or connected arrestable offence, and which is reasonably believed to be on the premises.
Police and Criminal Evidence Act	1984	Search premises after arrest for evidence	Police constable can, using reasonable force, enter premises where person was arrested, or which he had left shortly before arrest, to obtain evidence relating to the offence for which he was arrested, where there are reasonable grounds for believing it will be found on those premises.
Prevention of Terrorism Act	2005	Search for person to be made subject of control order and serve notice	Constable or person authorised by the Secretary of State may enter by force in order to serve order
Road Traffic Act	1988	Arrest person suspected of driving under influence of drink or drugs after accident has occurred in which reason to believe someone injured	Constable can enter any premises where he believes suspect to be found, if need be by force, in order to arrest him.
Telecommunications Act	1984	Seize equipment used in illegal broadcasting or evidence of related offences	Officers of OFCOM may seize property which is evidence of an offence reasonably believed to have been committed. Obstruction: £5,000 fine
Transport and Works Act	1992	Administer breath test to public transport staff, arrest for drunkenness	Police officer may enter any premises where person believed to be found who works on public transport, to administer breath test after accident in which injury believed to have occurred; may also enter to arrest on suspicion of being over alcohol limit, or for failure to provide a sample

TABLE TWO

POWERS REQUIRING A WARRANT TO BE OBTAINED

Act Title	Year	Purpose	Form/Requirements
Adoption and Children Act	2002	Search for child made subject of recovery order	Court order can authorise constable to enter by force and search for child. Obstruction: £1,000 fine
Arbitration Act	1996	Allows entry to take photographs and samples in support of arbitration proceedings	Need order from court (not arbitrating authority)
Asylum and Immigration (Treatment of Claimants, etc,) Act	2004	Enter to search for non-qualified provision of immigration advice or related services	Need warrant. Obstruction: £5,000 fine and/or maximum 6 months' imprisonment. Inserted powers into the Immigration and Asylum Act 1999.
Biological Weapons Act	1974	Inspect for offences related to supply and production of biological weapons	JP's warrant can authorise constable to enter and search premises, if necessary by force
Broadcasting Act	1990	Search for evidence of provision of unlicensed radio or television services	JP's warrant needed. Officer of OFCOM may enter and search. Obstruction: £5,000 fine
Children Act	1989	Search for child who has been made the subject of an Emergency Protection Order	Court must make EPO. Obstruction: £1,000 fine
Children Act	1989	Visit child subject to Supervision Order	Where child subject to supervision order, supervisor may enter premises where he/she is living in order to visit and supervise. Can get JP's search warrant authorising constable to enter by reasonable force if necessary.
Children and Young Persons (Harmful Publications) Act	1955	Search for materials used to produce "horror comics"	JP's warrant can authorise constable to enter and search for relevant materials, provided they relate to an alleged offence for which a summons has been issued
Children and Young Persons Act	1933	Check for child labour offences	JP's warrant can authorise constable to enter any premises at a reasonable time within 48 hours of the issue of the warrant. Obstruction: £500 fine
Children and Young Persons Act	1963	Inspect for child labour offences in relation to broadcasting and entertainment	Allowed powers under Children and Young Persons Act 1933 to be used on broadcasting studios, due to new restrictions on use of children in entertainment industry

POWERS REQUIRING A WARRANT TO BE OBTAINED

Act Title	Year	Purpose	Form/Requirements
Civil Procedure Act	1997	Inspect, search for, record and preserve evidence after application from party to action	High Court may make order, may authorise entry to premises. Entry to be supervised by experienced, neutral solicitor.
Communications Act	2003	Search for evidence of unlicensed TV watching	JP's warrant can give person authorised by the BBC or OFCOM authority to enter and search premises, if need be using reasonable force. Obstruction: £5,000 fine
Companies Act	1985	Search for and seize documents that have been required to be produced by the secretary of state; or which are evidence of an offence carrying at least 2 years' jail and which the secretary of state could have required to be produced	JP can issue warrant authorising force if either documents have not been produced in violation of Secretary of State's requirements, or evidence of crime. Entry to be effected by constables using reasonable force. Obstruction: unspecified fine
Competition Act	1998	Obtain evidence of restrictive trading, cartel offences or abuse of dominant market position	Officer authorised in writing by the Director-General of Fair Trading may enter without warrant business premises on which he has reason to believe may be found evidence of offences under the Competition Act or European law, after giving 2 working days' notice. Must get warrant to enter dwelling. Warrant can authorise force. Obstruction of entry under warrant: £5,000 fine
Computer Misuse Act	1990	Search for evidence of hacking	Circuit Judge may grant warrant after evidence on oath from constable that there is reason to believe a hacking offence is taking place or will take place on the premises and evidence of it could be found there. Warrant can authorise force.
Copyright, Designs and Patents Act	1988	Search for and seize evidence of criminal copyright infringement	JP may issue warrant authorising constable to enter using reasonable force
Copyright, etc. and Trade Marks (Offences and Enforcement) Act	2002	Search for evidence of dishonestly receiving transmissions for which payment is required (hacked satellite TV etc)	JP may issue warrant authorising constable to enter using reasonable force

POWERS REQUIRING A WARRANT TO BE OBTAINED

Act Title	Year	Purpose	Form/Requirements
County Courts Act	1984	Levy distress (seize goods in payment of debt)	Gives County Courts jurisdiction to grant "warrant of execution in the manner of *fieri facias*" in favour of winner of judgment, authorising levy of distress for rent. Is duty of constable to assist. Cannot generally use force against dwelling unless forcibly excluded.
Crime (Sentences) Act	1997	Search for offender liable to be arrested for breach of release supervision order	JP's warrant may authorise constable to enter and search premises, if need be using force, if satisfied that person or evidence related to breach of release supervision order to be found there
Criminal Damage Act	1971	Search for anything which has been used or is intended for use to destroy or damage property of another	JP may issue warrant, authorises constable to enter premises if need be by force to search
Criminal Justice (International Co-Operation) Act	1990	Search for evidence of offences committed outside the UK	JP may issue warrant on application of constable if satisfied that evidence relating to offence for which foreign court has laid charges, where that offence would be an arrestable offence if committed within the UK
Criminal Justice Act	1987	Seize documents required by serious fraud office	JP's warrant can authorise constable to enter by force and seize documents the production of which has been required by the Serious Fraud Office, but which have not been produced.
Criminal Justice Act	1988	Search for offensive weapons	JP may issue warrant on application by constable.
Criminal Justice and Police Act	2001	Enforce closure of premises selling unlicensed alcohol	Court must make closure order. Constable may enter at reasonable time using reasonable force to enforce the order. Obstruction: £5,000 fine or one month prison or both
Criminal Libel Act	1819	Seize blasphemous material	Court order can authorise constable to enter, by force if necessary, and seize copies of any material whose content constitutes blasphemous libel
Data Protection Act	1998	Search for evidence of violation of Data Protection Act	Warrant from circuit judge can authorise staff of the Information Commissioner to enter and search any premises, at a reasonable time unless that would compromise the search. Must give copy of warrant to occupier if present. Obstruction/unreasonable failure to assist: £5,000 fine
Dangerous Dogs Act	1991	Constable to enter and inspect for dangerous dogs	JP can issue warrant for constable to enter and search
Drug Trafficking Act	1994	Search for evidence of drug trafficking offences	Constable may apply to circuit judge for warrant, warrant authorises constable to enter and search
Emergency Laws (Re-enactments and Repeals) Act	1964	Seize documents relating to price controls on medical supplies and milk	JP's warrant can authorise entry by force if necessary to search for documents. Obstruction: £1,000 fine

POWERS REQUIRING A WARRANT TO BE OBTAINED

Act Title	Year	Purpose	Form/Requirements
Enterprise Act	2002	Office of fair trading to search for and seize documents	Office of Fair Trading official or official authorised by the OFT may enter with reasonable force with warrant from High Court judge. Warrant can be granted if reason to believe documents present which OFT could require to be produced
Extradition Act	2003	Arrest any person to be extradited, search for evidence of extradition offences	Constable or customs officer may enter and search if has reason to believe person to be arrested, or evidence of extradition offence on premises. Need warrant, which can be a foreign warrant if originating jurisdiction is designated as Category 1, else need domestic warrant to bring foreign warrant into effect. Can also search premises after arrest.
Finance Act	1976	HMRC search for evidence of tax/duty evasion	Inserted provisions into the Taxes Management Act 1970 allowing Circuit judge to grant order allowing entry by force if necessary. Must give warrant to occupier, or leave in prominent place if occupier absent.
Finance Act	2003	Investigate tax fraud	Need JP's warrant, must use within 14 days.
Financial Services and Markets Act	2000	Search for documents which Financial Services Authority could require to be produced	JP may issue warrant authorising constable to enter premises, if need be by force, if reason to believe that there are documents on the premises that the FSA investigator could require to be produced, and that they have not been produced or would be tampered with or destroyed if their production was required. Obstruction: £5,000 fine
Food and Environment Protection Act	1985	Inspect use of pesticides	Authorised officer of the Secretary of State or the Food Standards Agency may enter to inspect any premises where reason to believe pesticides kept. Need JP's warrant to enter dwelling.
Food and Environment Protection Act	1985	Inspect for presence of food unsuitable for human consumption, or evidence thereof	Officer of the Food Standards Agency may enter and search premises. Must have JP's warrant to enter a dwelling. Must enter at reasonable time unless that would frustrate the purpose of the search, and must show authority if asked.
Forgery and Counterfeiting Act	1981	Search for forged/counterfeit documents	JP's warrant can authorise constable to enter and search
Gaming (Bingo) Act	1985	Inspect for gambling offences related to bingo at licensed premises	Extended provisions of Gaming Act 1968 to bingo.
Gaming Act	1968	Inspect for gambling offences at licensed premises	If suspect gambling offences occurring at licensed premises, JP's warrant can authorise constable to enter and search at reasonable time.

POWERS REQUIRING A WARRANT TO BE OBTAINED

Act Title	Year	Purpose	Form/Requirements
Human Fertilisation and Embryology Act	1990	Search for evidence of offences under the act	JP's warrant can give officials of the Human Fertilisation and Embryology Authority power to enter, along with any constables, using reasonable force if necessary; if there are grounds to suspected that there is evidence on the premises of the commission of offences under the Act.
Immigration Act	1971	Arrest any person liable to detention under Immigration legislation	Constable may enter premises in order to effect arrest. Must get JP's warrant.
Incitement to Disaffection Act	1934	Search for evidence of attempt to seduce member(s) of HM forces away from their duty and allegiance	High Court Judge may grant warrant to police officer of rank of inspector or above to enter and search for evidence.
Indecent Displays (Control) Act	1981	Seize indecent material	JP's warrant can authorise constable to enter any premises where reason to suspect indecent displays present and seize any indecent material.
Knives Act	1997	Search for knives being sold in contravention of the Act	JP can issue warrant authorising constable to enter, using reasonable force if necessary
Landmines Act	1998	Search for evidence of offences against landmines prohibition	JP's warrant can authorise any person acting under the authority of the Secretary of State to enter and search any premises, using reasonable force. Obstruction: £5,000 fine
Local Government (Miscellaneous Provisions) Act	1982	Inspect premises where tattooing, acupuncture, ear piercing and electrolysis being carried out	Local authority officer must get JP's warrant in respect of premises where reason to believe tattooing, electrolysis, acupuncture or ear piercing is taking place in violation of licensing requirements. Must show authority if required. Obstruction: £1,000 fine
Lotteries and Amusements Act	1976	Search for evidence of gambling offences	JP may issue warrant if satisfied by information on oath that offences under the act being committed on any premises. Authorises constable to enter, search and seize documents, search any person present, and arrest anyone suspected of an offence.
Magistrates' Courts Act	1980	Seize goods in lieu of payment ordered by court	If person ordered to pay money by court and fails to do so, magistrates may issue warrant of distress authorising levy of distress against them.
Mental Health Act	1983	Detention and removal	Need JP's warrant, authorises constable to enter, search, detain and remove.
Merchant Shipping Act	1995	Search for illegally obtained items from shipwreck	If receiver has reason to believe that any wreck is in any house or on any land, he may apply to a JP for a warrant. Authorises entry, search and seizure

POWERS REQUIRING A WARRANT TO BE OBTAINED

Act Title	Year	Purpose	Form/Requirements
Misuse of Drugs Act	1971	Search for evidence of possession of controlled drugs	JP's warrant may authorise constable to enter by force and search for evidence
Nuclear Explosions (Prohibition and Inspection) Act	1998	Search for material or tools related to nuclear explosions	Need JP's warrant, authorisation by secretary of state. £5,000 fine for obstruction
Nuclear Safeguards Act	2000	Search for evidence or information relating to breaches of non-proliferation treaty	JP can issue warrant allowing constable to enter using reasonable force if necessary. Obstruction: £5,000 fine
Obscene Publications Act	1959	Search for obscene articles being kept for publication for gain	JP's warrant can authorise constable to enter and search for obscene material.
Offences Against the Person Act	1861	Search for offensive weapons/explosives/ dangerous substances	JP's search warrant authorises entry and search by constable of premises where reasonable cause to believe any dangerous substance kept, or any instrument intended to be used to commit an offence under the Act
Official Secrets Act	1911	Search for material related to breach of official secrets	JP's warrant may authorise constable to enter and search, if satisfied that offence under the act has been or will be committed. In "great emergency", where immediate action necessary to safeguard interests of the state, police superintendent may authorise in lieu of JP.
Petroleum (Consolidation) Act	1928	Search for evidence of illegal sale of petrol	Warrant from magistrates' court authorises any person named in the warrant to enter and search for evidence
Police and Criminal Evidence Act	1984	Search premises for evidence of serious arrestable offence	JP's warrant may authorise constable to enter premises using reasonable force, and search for evidence likely to assist in the investigation of a serious arrestable offence. For privileged or special procedure material, must have warrant from circuit judge.
Proceeds of Crime Act	2002	Search for evidence of benefit from crime	Officer of Assets Recovery Agency can apply to judge of sufficient jurisdiction to exercise authority over Crown Court or above for a warrant, which authorises entry and search if reason to believe material on the premises useful to investigation.
Protection of Children Act	1978	Search for indecent photographs of children	JP's warrant may authorise constable to enter and search premises and seize any indecent photographs, if reason to believe they are on the premises.
Public Order Act	1936	Search for evidence of organisation or training of quasi-military group	JP's warrant can authorise any person named in it, and any other police officers, to enter and search and seize any evidence.

POWERS REQUIRING A WARRANT TO BE OBTAINED

Act Title	Year	Purpose	Form/Requirements
Public Order Act	1986	Search for racially inflammatory material	JP may issue warrant if satisfied that reasonable grounds to suspect possession of racially inflammatory material. Warrant authorises constable to enter and search, using reasonable force..
Public Stores Act	1875	Search for and seize stores diverted from public property	JP's warrant may authorise constable to search for and seize stores from which marks denoting Her Majesty's property have been obliterated.
Social Security Act	1998	Seize goods in lieu of contribution, interest or other penalty	JP can issue warrant authorising entry by force if necessary to seize goods which can then be sold. Constable may assist. Amends Social Security Administration act 1992 to bring this into effect.
Terrorism Act	2000	Search for evidence of terrorist offences	JP's warrant can authorise constable to enter and search premises where reason to believe terrorist evidence to be found
Terrorism Act	2000	Arrest terror suspect	JP's warrant can authorise constable to enter any premises in order to arrest a person suspected of carrying out or plotting terror acts
Theatres Act	1968	Observe play being performed at any premises to document obscenity, racist material, incitement to crime etc	JP can issue warrant where reasonable grounds to suspect that play being performed involving commission of offences against the Act. Warrant allows constable to enter to attend performance.
Theft Act	1968	Search for stolen goods	JP's warrant may authorised named constable to enter premises and search for stolen goods or goods obtained by deception, blackmail etc.
Video Recordings Act	1984	Inspect for offences related to classification and censorship of video recordings	JP's warrant may authorise constable to enter and search where reasonable grounds to believe that an offence has been committed on the premises and that evidence is to be found there.
Wireless Telegraphy Act	1949	Inspect for offences against broadcasting regulations, or interference with broadcasting	Must get JP's warrant, which authorises named OFCOM officers to enter premises named in the warrant, if necessary by force. Obstruction: £5,000 fine

TABLE THREE

POWERS ALLOWING IMMEDIATE ENTRY, WHERE A WARRANT IS AVAILABLE

Act Title	Year	Purpose	Form/Requirements
Agriculture and Horticulture Act	1964	Inspect horticultural produce for false/incorrect grading	Inspector appointed by Secretary of State may enter at any reasonable time upon production of authority, provided premises not used only as a dwelling. JP's warrant can authorise force. Obstruction: £1,000 fine
Animal Health Act	2002	Inspect for presence of specified disease in livestock	Inspector may enter any premises at any time to tak samples and perform tests to discover if foot-and-mouth disease or any other disease specified by the Minister is present on the premises. Can get JP's warrant authorising reasonable force. Obstruction: £5,000 fine for 1st offence, £5,000 fine and/or 1 month prison for subsequent offences
Animal Health Act	2002	Slaughter animals in order to control disease	Inserted provisions into Animal Health Act 1981. Inspector may enter to decide whether to slaughter animals, and to carry out slaughter. Can get JP's warrant to use reasonable force. Obstruction: £5,000 fine for first offence, £5,000 fine and/or 1 month prison for subsequent offences
Betting and Gaming Duties Act	1981	Check for evasion of bingo duty or duty or violation of amusement machine licence requirements	Customs officer can enter any premises where reason to believe Bingo/amusement machines being played. JP's warrant can authorise force
Building Act	1984	Ascertain level of compliance with building regulations, carry out necessary work	24 hours' notice, show authority if required. Must carry out at reasonable time. JP's warrant can authorise force. Obstruction: £200 fine
Caravan Sites and Control of Development Act	1960	To inspect a caravan site, check for compliance with local authority's standards and terms of licensing of site, decide what conditions to impose or vary	No warrant needed, enter at reasonable hour after giving 24 hours' notice. Can get warrant if force needed. Must give notice. Obstruction: £200 fine
Childcare Act	2006	Can enter premises where childcare suspected of being provided in contravention of licensing requirements	Any person authorised by the Chief Inspector of Schools may enter any premises at a reasonable time to inspect. Can get JP's warrant for force. Constable may accompany when entering under warrant.

POWERS ALLOWING IMMEDIATE ENTRY, WHERE A WARRANT IS AVAILABLE

Act Title	Year	Purpose	Form/Requirements
Care Standards Act	2000	Inspect childcare provision	Inserted provisions into the Children Act 1989. Inspector authorised by HM Chief Inspector of Schools may enter any premises where childcare provided, or where reason to believe it is being provided in contravention of the Act. Can get JP's search warrant authorising constable to enter by force if necessary.
Children Act	1989	Inspect premises where fostered children looked after or proposed to be looked after	Local authority inspector may enter at any reasonable time on showing authority. No obstruction offence. Can get JP's search warrant authorising constable to enter by reasonable force if necessary
Clean Air Act	1993	Inspect fireplace if house within smoke control area, decide if needs to be modified to reduce pollution	Must give seven days' notice and show authority. Can get warrant to authorise force. Obstruction: £1,000 fine
Clean Neighbourhoods and Environment Act	2005	Switch off noisy intruder alarm	Alarm must have been sounding continuously for 20 mins or intermittently for 1 hour, must be reasonable cause for annoyance. Reasonable effort must be made to get keyholder to shut it down if premises in designated Notification Area. May enter to shut down alarm, JP's warrant can authorise reasonable force. Must leave notice at premises before seeking warrant
Coast Protection Act	1949	Carry out work to prevent coastal erosion	Local authorities in coastal areas may enter to carry out sea defence works, or inspect to determine whether such work should be done. Must show authority and give 24 hours' notice. JP's warrant can authorise force. Obstruction: £1,000 fine
Consumer Protection Act	1987	Inspect for violations of product labelling/safety requirements	Local trading standards officers may enter to inspect at any reasonable time, provided premises not used only as a dwelling. JP's warrant can authorise force. Obstruction: £5,000 fine
Control of Pollution Act	1974	Exercise or decide whether to exercise powers related to noise pollution	Officer authorised in writing by local authority may enter on production of authority. Must give 7 days' notice to enter residential property unless in emergency. Can get JP's warrant to authorise force. Obstruction: £1,000 fine.
Diseases of Fish Act	1937	Inspect fish for disease	Inspector appointed by Minister can enter any land on production of his authority to take samples of fish. If none are found to be infected, must pay market rate for the sample. Warrant available, but no mention of force. Obstruction: £2,500 fine

POWERS ALLOWING IMMEDIATE ENTRY, WHERE A WARRANT IS AVAILABLE

Act Title	Year	Purpose	Form/Requirements
Electricity Act	1989	Survey land to determine its suitability for use in connection with supply of electricity	Authorised officer of electricity supplier may enter. Must give 14 days' notice. Cannot be used against land covered by a building or by planning permission for a building. Can get JP's warrant to authorise reasonable force. Obstruction: £1,000 fine.
Environmental Protection Act	1990	To remedy non-compliance with statutory nuisance Abatement Notice	24 hours' notice, JP's warrant can authorise force. Obstruction: £1,000 fine
Explosives Act	1875	Search for explosives	JP's warrant can authorise entry to search for explosives. If there is a danger to life and a delay to seek a warrant would be too dangerous, an officer of the rank of Superintendent or above can authorise entry. Obstruction: unlimited fine
Finance Act	1991	Search premises used in connection with a business for purposes connected with excise duty	Can get JP's warrant if entry refused. Warrant can authorise force. Warrant issued if JP satisfied that there is evidence of a serious fraud offence being carried out at the premises
Finance Act	1994	Inspect for evidence of serious fraud related to Insurance Premium Tax	Customs officer can at any reasonable time enter premises containing goods subject to customs charges, provided premises concerned with the business of importing, selling or otherwise dealing with the goods
Finance Act	1997	Inspect premises where activities subject to Gaming Duty taking place	Can enter without warrant, or can get warrant for force. Also amends Customs and Excise Management Act to include gaming duty
Food Safety Act	1990	Check for food safety violations	Local authority inspector can enter any premises. Must give 24 hours' notice and produce authority. Can get JP's warrant to authorise force. Obstruction: £5,000 fine or 3 months' prison
Gas Act	1965	To examine, drill etc. to discover any underground site suitable to be used for the storage of gas.	Must give 28 days' notice. Entry if consent within notice period, else can get warrant. Obstruction: £200 fine
Gas Act	1995	Multiple purposes connected with supply of gas, inspecting equipment, meter inspections, testing quality, removing meter	Must have written authority and show on request. Can get JP's warrant in accordance with the Rights of Entry (Gas and Electricity Boards) Act 1954. Must give 24 hours' notice if disconnecting supply or removing meter. Obstruction: £1,000 fine

POWERS ALLOWING IMMEDIATE ENTRY, WHERE A WARRANT IS AVAILABLE

Act Title	Year	Purpose	Form/Requirements
Highways Act	1980	Inspect land for any purpose connected to Highways Agency's functions; repair/maintain equipment, signs etc	Must have written authority and produce if required. Give 7 days' notice if land occupied. If entry refused can get magistrates' court order, granting entry 9am-6pm. Obstruction: £1,000 fine
Housing Act	1985	Measure rooms to regulate overcrowding	Inspector authorised in writing may enter at any reasonable time after giving 24 hours' notice. Can get JP's warrant to authorise force.
Housing Act	2004	Ascertain compliance with housing standards or improvement order	24 hours' notice. Obstruction: £2,500 fine Can get JP's warrant.
Medicines Act	1968	Inspect for violation of medicines regulations or accuracy of statements on licence application	Inspector authorised by Secretary of State may enter at any reasonable time on production of his authority. Must give 24 hour's notice before entering premises used only as a dwelling. Can get JP's warrant authorising force.
Mineral Workings Act	1985	Reclaim or carry out improvements to land that has been used for underground mining, other than coal mining	Any person authorised by local authority may enter to survey land or carry out works. Must give 10 days' notice. JP's warrant can authorise force or entry to land where occupiers cannot be contacted. Obstruction: £1,000 fine
Noise Act	1996	Fast-track entry procedures to deal with noise nuisance being caused at night	Local authority officer can enter to seize stereos etc where noise exceeds level permitted in warning notice. Can get JP's warrant, which can authorise force. Obstruction: £1,000 fine
Pensions Act	1995	Inspect for breaches of occupational pensions management rules	Officer of the Occupational Pensions Regulatory Authority may enter and inspect any premises where beneficiaries of occupational pension scheme employed, or where scheme is being managed or documents related to scheme kept. Dwellings can be inspected as long as used for business purposes. Must show authority. Can get warrant authorising reasonable force, apply to JP. Obstruction: £5,000 fine
Planning (Hazardous Substances) Act	1990	Inspect land to decide whether to make Hazardous Substances Contravention Notice or exercise related powers	Officer of a Hazardous Substances undertaker or Secretary of State may enter at any reasonable time. Must show authority, 24 hours' notice for occupied land. Obstruction: £1000 fine. Can get JP's warrant.
Planning and Compensation Act	1991	Inspect for breach of planning controls and exercise any related powers	If action not taken within period of compliance with notice, employees of the planning authority (local authority) may enter and carry out works. Can get JP's warrant. Obstruction: £1,000 fine. Amends Town and Country Planning Act 1990

POWERS ALLOWING IMMEDIATE ENTRY, WHERE A WARRANT IS AVAILABLE

ct Title	Year	Purpose	Form/Requirements
'roperty 1isdescriptions Act	1991	Search for evidence of misdescriptions of property in relation to estate agency or property development business	Officer of local Weights and Measures Authority may enter premises at a reasonable time to inspect for evidence of offence. Can get warrant from JP authorising force. Can be used against dwellings only if also used for business purposes.
'ublic Health (Control f Disease) Act	1984	Test persons for notifiable disease	24 hours' notice, can get warrant. Obstruction: £1,000 fine
'ublic Health Act	1936	Inspect for any breach of the Act or bylaws made under it, carry out any work necessary to remedy the situation	Local authority officer can enter at any reasonable time, showing authority. Must give 24 hours' notice in writing. Can get JP's warrant to authorise force. Obstruction: £200 fine
'ublic Health Act	1936	Cleansing of Verminous Persons	Must give 24 hours' notice to occupier. Magistrates' court order may authorise force
ladioactive Material Road Transport) Act	1991	Inspect for any vehicle used to transport radioactive material and check whether vehicle complies with relevant standards	Inspector appointed by Secretary of State may enter at reasonable time upon production of authority. Warrant can authorise reasonable force. Obstruction: £1,000 fine
crap Metal Dealers ct	1964	Check for unlicensed scrap metal dealing	Local authority inspector may enter to see if premises being used to deal scrap metal without registration. Can get JP's warrant to use force. Obstruction: £200 fine
laughterhouses Act	1974	Inspect premises licensed as a slaughterhouse or knacker's yard	Officer authorised in writing may enter premises at any reasonable time, but must give 24 hours' notice to enter dwelling. Can get warrant to authorise force. Obstruction: £1,000 fine and/or 1 month prison. Failure to assist: £200 fine.
ourts and Legal ervices Act	1990	Check for offences related to unqualified persons practising as solicitors	Inserted entry powers into Solicitors Act 1974, to examine for evidence of offences under the 1974 Act. Officer of local weights and measures authority may enter and premises not used solely as a dwelling at any reasonable time and on production of his authority. Can get JP's warrant for force. Obstruction: £1000 fine
axes Management Act	1970	Levy distress for unpaid taxes	Tax collector may enter in order to remove goods in lieu of unpaid taxes. Can get warrant from JP authorising forcible entry, assisted by constables if necessary.
obacco Advertising nd Promotion Act	2002	Search for evidence of tobacco advertising offences	Inspector can enter at any reasonable time to check for evidence of tobacco advertising. JP's warrant can authorise force. Can be used against dwellings only if used for business purposes. Obstruction: £1,000 fine

POWERS ALLOWING IMMEDIATE ENTRY, WHERE A WARRANT IS AVAILABLE

Act Title	Year	Purpose	Form/Requirements
Trade Descriptions Act	1968	Check for offences against Trade Descriptions Acts.	Officers of local weights and measures authority may enter any premises not used solely as a dwelling at any reasonable time to check for offences. Can be used to "spot check". JP's warrant can authorise entry where there is reasonable grounds to believe there are items on the premises which the officer would be entitled to inspect, and that they are likely to be evidence of an offence.
Utilities Act	2000	Inspect electrical kit used in supply, repair kit, remove meter, general inspections related to electricity supply	Entry at reasonable time. JP's warrant can authorise force. Obstruction: £1,000 fine. Amends Electricity Act 1989
Value Added Tax Act	1994	Inspect carrying on of any activities liable to VAT	Authorised person may enter at reasonable time. JP's warrant can authorise force if reason to believe serious fraud taking place there.
Water Industry Act	1991	Enforce hosepipe ban	Person designated by water undertaker may enter to inspect. Must give 24 hours' notice. Can get JP's warrant to authorise force. Obstruction: £200 fine.
Water Industry Act	1991	Investigate contamination of water sources	Person designated by water undertaker may enter to inspect. Must give 24 hours' notice. Can get JP's warrant to authorise force. Obstruction: £200 fine.
Water Industry Act	1991	Carry out any surveys, inspections or any powers or water undertaker; monitor quality of drinking water	Applies of officials of water undertaker. 24 hours' notice, entry during reasonable hours. JP's warran[t] can authorise force. Can enter immediately if emergency. Obstruction: £1,000 fine
Water Industry Act	1991	Powers in connection with installation and use of water meters	Water undertaker personnel may enter. Must give 24 hours' notice and show authority. Entry at reasonable time. Can get JP's warrant to authorise force. Obstruction: £1,000 fine
Water Industry Act	1991	Check for any violation of sewerage rules (e.g. trade effluent), carry out any necessary works	Sewerage undertaker may enter any premises to inspect or carry out works. Must give 24 hours' notice and show authority. Can get warrant to use force from JP. Obstruction: £200 fine
Water Industry Act	1991	Monitor quality of water supplied by undertaker	Officer of local authority or DEFRA may enter any premises to test quality of water supplied to it by water undertaker. Must show authority and give 2[4] hours' notice. Can get JP's warrant to authorise force. Obstruction: £1,000 fine

POWERS ALLOWING IMMEDIATE ENTRY, WHERE A WARRANT IS AVAILABLE

Act Title	Year	Purpose	Form/Requirements
Water Industry Act	1991	Monitor waste of water, enforce court order for sealing of well	Authorised officer of Environment Agency or local authority may enter to inspect or seal well pursuant to court order. Must show authority if asked and give 24 hours' notice. Can get JP's warrant for force. Obstruction: £200 fine
Water Resources Act	1991	Survey land to decide whether to carry out work related to water resources; drill and search for water, sample water; lay pipes or carry out other works	Must have written authorisation and give seven days' notice except in case of emergency. JP's warrant can authorise force. Obstruction: £1,000 fine.
Weights and Measures Act	1985	Inspect equipment used for weighing and measuring in the course of business	Local weights and measures officer can enter premises not used solely as a dwelling at all reasonable times on production of authority, Can get JP's warrant to authorise use of reasonable force. Obstruction: £5,000 fine
Welfare Reform and Pensions Act	1999	Search for documents relating to administration of pension scheme	Inspector may enter at reasonable time. Must show authorisation if asked. Can get warrant for force. Inserts these powers into the Pension Schemes Act 1993.

TABLE FOUR

POWERS ALLOWING IMMEDIATE ENTRY, WHERE NO WARRANT IS AVAILABLE

Act Title	Year	Purpose	Form/Requirements
Adoption and Children Act	2002	Inspect premises where adopted child living or in respect of which notice of intention to adopt lodged	Must show written authorisation from minister. Obstruction: £1,000 fine
Agricultural Marketing Act	1958	Inspect agricultural produce	Must have written authorisation from Secretary of Sta
Agricultural Wages Act	1948	Investigate circumstances of agricultural wages dispute	Minister may appoint officers, treasury must consent number. Officer may enter at reasonable times with reasonable notice. Obstruction: £1,000 fine
Agriculture Act	1947	Multi-purpose entry power for inspections	Authorisation by Minister. 24 hours' notice required. Must produce authority if required. Obstruction: £500 fine or £1,000 if obstruct carrying out of works.
Agriculture Act	1967	Inspect premises used for slaughter of livestock or packing/cutting of meat	Authorised officer of Meat and Livestock Commissio has power to enter at any reasonable time any premises not used solely as a dwelling. Obstruction: £200 fine
Agriculture Act	1967	Official of Rural Development board deciding if/how to exercise board's powers	Entry at reasonable time, must produce authority if asked, must give 7 days' notice. Obstruction: £200 fi
Agriculture Act	1970	Obtain information in connection with scheme for the eradication of Brucellosis	DEFRA officer authorised in writing by the Secretary State may enter any land or premises at any reasonable time. Must produce authority if required. Obstruction: £1,000 fine and/or 1 month prison
Agriculture Act	1970	Inspections of fertilisers for sale	Inspector appointed by local authority may premises reason to believe fertiliser being kept there for sale. May also enter if reason to believe recently purchase fertiliser on site, if premises not purely a dwelling. Mu show written authority. Obstruction: £1,000 fine
Alcoholic Liquor Duties Act	1979	Inspect for fraud related to denatured alcohol	Customs officer may enter premises of any person authorised by regulations under the Act to receive denatured alcohol. Must pay a reasonable price for a samples taken.

POWERS ALLOWING IMMEDIATE ENTRY, WHERE NO WARRANT IS AVAILABLE

Title	Year	Purpose	Form/Requirements
ient Monuments and ıaeological Areas Act	1979	Inspect ancient monuments, assess effects of proposed works on monuments	Inspector appointed by Secretary of State may enter to inspect for presence of monument believed to exist, or to assess likely effects of proposed works on scheduled monument. Must give 24 hours' notice to enter occupied land, no entry to dwelling without permission. Obstruction: £1,000 fine
nal Boarding ablishments Act	1963	Inspect kennels/cattery etc	Inspector appointed by local authority may enter any premises licensed under the Act at any reasonable time on production of authority. Obstruction: £500 fine
nal Health Act	1981	Protect poultry from suffering	Inspector may enter any premises on which he has reason to believe poultry is being kept in order to examine; if an order for the prevention of suffering to poultry has been made. Obstruction: £5,000 fine for first offence, £5,000 fine and/or 1 month prison for subsequent offences
nal Health Act	1981	Inspect to see if animal carrying zoonosis (animal disease transmissible to humans) is or has been on premises, order steps to be taken to prevent disease	Veterinary inspector may enter any premises if he has reason to believe that animal affected by designated disease is or has been there. Must show authority where required. Obstruction: £5,000 fine for first offence, £5,000 fine and/or 1 month prison for subsequent offences
nal Health Act	1981	Destroy wild animals in order to prevent spread of disease	Authorised officer may enter at any time to inspect if there is reason to believe that a disease of wild animals to which the Section applies exists. If order made, can also enter to destroy members of species, erect fences, inspect to see if destruction carried out properly. Power to enter for inspection continues for 2 years after revocation of order. May be used against private land but not dwelling. Obstruction: £5,000 fine for first offence, £5,000 fine and/or 1 month prison for subsequent offences.
nal Health Act	1981	Inspections related to Minister's powers to spend money on eradication of animal disease (broader than livestock)	Veterinary inspector or other officer authorised in writing by the Minister may enter any land or premises at any reasonable time to take samples. Must produce authority on demand. Obstruction: £1,000 fine and/or 1 month prison
nal Health Act	1981	Ascertain whether any regulation implementing a requirement of European law is being infringed	Inspector may enter any land or premises at any reasonable time to inspect. Inserted by the Animal Health Act 1981 (Amendment) Regulations 1992

POWERS ALLOWING IMMEDIATE ENTRY, WHERE NO WARRANT IS AVAILABLE

Act Title	Year	Purpose	Form/Requirements
Animal Health Act	1981	Destroy foxes or other wild mammals in area designated as infected with Rabies	Minister has power to make order for destruction. Order may authorise any person to enter any land, including private land but not including a dwelling. Obstruction: £5,000 fine for first offence, £5,000 fine and/or 1 month prison for subsequent offences.
Animal Health Act	1981	Inspect for animal disease or illegally imported animals	Veterinary inspector or person authorised by the Secretary of State may enter at any reasonable time reason to believe disease on site or regulations of Minister flouted, showing reasons in writing if requested. May enter at any time without restrictions check for disease or illegally imported animals. Obstruction: £5,000 fine for first offence, £5,000 fine and/or 1 month prison for subsequent offences
Anti-Social Behaviour Act	2003	Carry out work on graffiti	Entry may take place 28 days after the service of a Defacement Removal Notice, if the required work ha not been undertaken.
Anti-Social Behaviour Act	2003	Inspection of high hedges to decide whether or not Remedial Notice should be imposed/varied.	Must show authorisation if requested. 24 hours' noti Obstruction: £1,000 fine
Bees Act	1980	Check for the presence of foreign bees	Must show authority if asked. Obstruction: £1,000 fir
British Waterways Act	1995	Entry to carry out works for the maintenance of waterways	Written authorisation needed. Must give 28 days' notice. In emergency, may enter immediately but m inform occupier as soon as possible of what has bee done, and serve formal written notice within 7 days c entry. Obstruction: £2,500 fine for emergency entry, £500 for non-emergency.
Child Support Act	1991	Inspect any premises where non-resident parent working, or where information held about that person which was acquired in the course of a business	Secretary of State may authorise inspectors, who m enter and inspect after showing authority if required. Obstruction: £1,000 fine
Children and Young Persons Act	1969	Arrest juvenile remanded into local authority care	Police officer may enter without warrant to arrest an young person who has been remanded or committe into local authority care

POWERS ALLOWING IMMEDIATE ENTRY, WHERE NO WARRANT IS AVAILABLE

Title	Year	Purpose	Form/Requirements
l Aviation Act	1982	Erect signs indicating danger to aircraft, or survey land preparatory to exercise of this power.	Secretary of State can authorise proprietor of licensed aerodrome to carry out the work. Must give 2 months' notice of intention, then a further 14 days before work starts. If objection received, Secretary of State must authorise the work. Obstruction: £1,000 fine. For survey power, need 24 hours' notice, must show authority. Obstruction: £500 fine
npulsory Purchase	1965	Inspect land prior to compulsory purchase	Must give not less than 3 and not more than 14 days' notice. Compulsory Purchase Order must have been made.
ıservation of Seals	1970	Survey seal populations, cull seals	Secretary of State may authorise entry to survey seal population or cull seals which are damaging fish stocks. Must give 48 hours' notice for inspection, or 28 days for proposed cull. Obstruction: £2,500 fine
ıntryside Act	1968	Survey land to decide whether to exercise powers related to footpaths	Extends powers under National Parks and Access to the Countryside Act 1949 to cover surveys for footpath functions. Inspector must be authorised in writing by the Secretary of State and produce authority before entering if required. Obstruction: £200 fine
ıntryside and Rights Vay Act	2000	"Right to Roam" of general public. Also inspections related to enforcement/promotion of right to roan	Anyone can wander onto land appearing on a map as open country. Also authorised officials of several agencies, e.g. National Parks service, Forestry Commission, have right to enter to inspect and decide how/whether to exercise powers and duties conferred on them by the Act.
ninal Justice and lic Order Act	1994	Find out whether rave in progress or being prepared on land and seize equipment	If police officer of rank of at least Superintendent believes circumstances exist which would justify him giving directions under the act forbidding a rave, a constable may enter without a warrant to find out if that is the case, or seize anything required to be removed by those directions
toms and Excise ıagement Act	1979	Prevent signalling to smugglers	Customs officer, constable, coastguard or member of the armed forces may enter any house or other property where reason to believe signal being sent or about to be sent to smugglers and take necessary steps to stop it.
toms and Excise ıagement Act	1979	Access pipeline through which dutiable substance flows	Customs officer may cross land adjacent to pipeline in order to get to and from pipeline.
ıgerous Wild Animals	1976	Inspect premises where dangerous wild animal kept or proposed to be kept	Inspector can enter at any reasonable time and premises licensed to keep dangerous wild animals, or which have applied for a licence. Must produce authority. Obstruction: £5,000 fine

POWERS ALLOWING IMMEDIATE ENTRY, WHERE NO WARRANT IS AVAILABLE

Act Title	Year	Purpose	Form/Requirements
Distress for Rent Act	1689	Landlord seizing household goods in lieu of unpaid rent	Landlord may enter tenant's dwelling without warran No force allowed but in practice difficult to prevent
Dogs Act	1906	Seize stray dog	Constable can enter land to seize any dog appearin be a stray. Need permission to enter private land.
Endangered Species (Import and Export) Act	1976	Check legality of imported plants	Authorisation by Secretary of State, may enter at reasonable time. Must produce authority if asked. Obstruction: £1,000 fine.
Environmental Protection Act	1990	Remove abandoned luggage or shopping trolley	Entry only with consent, or "deemed consent" where objection received after notice served
Fire Precautions Act	1971	Carry out inspections of premises requiring fire certificate or similar	Must show written authority if asked. 24 hours' notic required to enter premises used as a dwelling. Obstruction: £1,000 fine
Forestry Act	1967	Inspect timber	Forestry Commission may make order conferring authority, which must be shown if asked. Obstructio £1,000 fine
Forestry Act	1967	Haul timber to road from forest	Landowner must be given opportunity to be heard o the subject before order made
Game Laws (Amendment) Act	1960	Inspect for poaching offences	Constable may enter land where reasonable ground to suspect poaching offence being committed
Gas Act	1986	Emergency entry to check for/counteract gas leak	Officer of Gas supplier can enter immediately on production of his authority if reason to believe gas escaping. Must give notice explaining what done an why within 5 working days of entry.
Gas Act	1965	Enquire into accident	Tribunal set up to enquire into gas accident may authorise inspector to enter any place or building if necessary for the purposes of the accident enquiry.
Geological Survey Act	1845	Natural Environment Research Council can enter to survey land.	Must be at reasonable time of day, notice must be given. Obstruction: £20 fine
Goods Vehicles (Licensing of Operators) Act	1995	Inspect vehicle or consignment note	Officer of local traffic commissioner or police consta may enter any premises where goods vehicle or consignment note held and inspect/copy. Obstructio £1,000 fine
Health and Safety At Work Etc Act	1974	General purpose entry power for inspectors of the Health and Safety Executive and local authorities	Can enter any premises that he has reason to believ he needs to enter in order to carry out his functions. Constable may accompany. Obstruction: £5,000 fine

POWERS ALLOWING IMMEDIATE ENTRY, WHERE NO WARRANT IS AVAILABLE

t Title	Year	Purpose	Form/Requirements
l Farming Act	1946	Inspect for compliance with law on keeping of rams, burning of grassland heather and other Hill Farming related activities.	Officer of DEFRA may enter at any reasonable time to inspect on production of authority. Obstruction: £500 fine
ousing Act	1985	Carry out repairs required by repair notice but not done	Local authority workmen can enter to carry out repairs required in Repair Notice that has not been complied with. Obstruction (including presence of owner's own workmen): £1,000 fine plus recovery of any expenses.
ousing Act	1985	Inspect for purposes of making of Control Order for multiple occupation premises, or carry out works related to the Order	Entry may be effected at any time by anyone authorised in writing by the local authority. If person refuses to allow works to be carried out, can get magistrates' court order commanding him to permit entry. If breached, £5,000 fine.
ousing Act	1985	Cleanse premises of vermin where premises subject to Demolition Order	Where demolition order made and it appears to the authority that the premises need to be cleansed of vermin, may serve written notice of intention to cleanse. May enter once premises vacated.
ousing Act	1985	General power to inspect houses owned by local authority	All houses owned by local authority must be open to inspection by that authority at any time.
ousing Act	1985	General survey powers to decide whether to exercise other powers, e.g. repair notice	Must have written authority from Secretary of State or local authority. Notice requirements vary between 24 hours and 7 days depending on purpose. Obstruction: £1,000 fine.
'pnotism Act	1952	Check for offences related to stage hypnotism	Constable may enter any premises where entertainments are being held if reason to believe any offences against the Act are being or may be committed there
ıeritance Tax Act	1984	Inheritance Tax valuations	Person authorised by the Board of HMRC may enter to value property for inheritance tax purposes. Occupier must permit entry. Obstruction: £200 fine
ernational Carriage of erishable Foodstuffs t	1976	Inspect vehicle used to transport perishable foodstuffs	Inspector may at any reasonable time and on production of authority enter any premises where reason to believe vehicle subject to Certificate of Compliance or Certification Plate kept, and inspect. Obstruction: £1,000 fine

POWERS ALLOWING IMMEDIATE ENTRY, WHERE NO WARRANT IS AVAILABLE

Act Title	Year	Purpose	Form/Requirements
Land Drainage Act	1991	Inspect land for any purposes related to the functions of the National Rivers Authority or drainage boards – assessing drainage etc	Must show authority, need to give seven days' notice case of dwelling, unless emergency. Obstruction: £2,500 fine
Law of Distress Amendment Act	1888	Levy distress for debt	Certified bailiff may enter to levy distress for debt on behalf of creditor. Refined pre-existing common-law power
Local Government (Miscellaneous Provisions) Act	1976	Survey land with view to compulsory purchase	Must have written authority from local authority, give 1 days' notice and enter at reasonable time. Obstructio £1,000 fine
Local Government (Miscellaneous Provisions) Act	1976	Inspect to decide whether to issue notice requiring work to be carried out on tree	Inspector authorised by local authority may enter to inspect tree. Must show authority. Obstruction: £1,00 fine
Local Government (Miscellaneous Provisions) Act	1982	Enforce covenant binding successor in title to land	Must give 21 days' notice to anyone with an interest in the land bound by the covenant. May then enter and carry out work required by covenant, and recover expenses against person bound.
Local Government (Miscellaneous Provisions) Act	1982	Carry out work to secure vacant property from trespassers or prevent it threatening public health	Must give 48 hours' notice to occupier, unless impossible to locate them or case is too urgent. Notice can be appealed in County Court. After notice period any person authorised by local authority may enter to carry out the work. Can recover expenses person to whom notice given or could have been given.
Local Government and Housing Act	1989	Inspect housing to decide if any powers of local authority should be exercised, or value for putative compulsory purchase	Need written authority from Secretary of State or local authority, must give 7 days' notice. Obstruction: £1,00 fine
Local Government Finance Act	1988	Valuations of hereditaments in relation to council tax non-domestic rating	Must give 24 hours' notice, show authorisation. Obstruction: £200 fine
Local Government Finance Act	1992	Valuation for purposes of council tax lists	Must give 3 clear days' notice, not including weekend Christmas Day, Good Friday or Bank Holidays. Must produce authority if required. Obstruction: £500 fine
Local Government Planning and Land Act	1980	Survey ahead of compulsory acquisition by Urban Development Corporation	Officer of the Urban Development Corporation or the Valuation Office of HMRC may enter land proposed to be acquired at any reasonable time upon 28 days' notice. Obstruction: £1,000 fine

POWERS ALLOWING IMMEDIATE ENTRY, WHERE NO WARRANT IS AVAILABLE

Title	Year	Purpose	Form/Requirements
k (Cessation of ›duction) Act	1985	Check if recipient of compensation for milk producers exiting the market is fraudulently still producing	Officer authorised by the Secretary of State may enter any land occupied by a person to whom payment made at any reasonable time to inspect. Obstruction: £5,000 fine.
suse of Drugs Act	1971	Inspect premises of supplier of controlled drugs	Police constable may enter premises at any time to inspect stocks of drugs and any documentation. Obstruction: £5,000 fine and/or 2 years prison
tional Assistance Act	1948	Take into safe storage belongings of person in hospital	Entry at reasonable time, must produced ID where asked. Obstruction: £2,500 fine
tional Health Service d Community Care Act	1990	Inspect premises where any person receives care in the community	Must show authorisation where requested. Obstruction: £1,000 fine
tional Heritage Act	1983	Inspect and catalogue ancient monument or check if one exists	Written authorisation from Historic Buildings and Monuments Commission ("English Heritage"). No entry to occupied land without 24 hours' notice, no entry to dwelling without permission. Obstruction: £1,000 fine
tional Minimum Wage	1998	Inspect for failure to pay national minimum wage	May enter at any reasonable time to inspect records if premises used for business purposes. Obstruction: £5,000 fine
tional Parks and cess to the untryside Act	1949	Inspection for territory suitable for inclusion in national park	Must give 14 days' notice and show authority if requested. Obstruction: £200 fine.
dnance Survey Act	1841	Carry out Ordnance Survey	Must give written notice of intent. Obstruction: £200 fine
ty Wall, etc. Act	1996	Entry to carry out maintenance work on party wall.	Owner/occupier of adjacent premises needing to carry out work may enter. Must be during reasonable hours, 14 days' notice required. Obstruction: £1,000 fine
forming Animals egulation) Act	1925	Inspect premises where animals trained	Constable or authorised local authority officer may enter any premises where performing animals are kept or trained at any reasonable time. Obstruction: £1,000 fine
sts Act	1954	To inspect for the presence of rabbits and for compliance with a Rabbit Clearance Order	Authorisation by Minister, must be at reasonable time
Animals Act	1951	Inspect pet shop	Veterinary surgeon or officer of local authority may enter any licensed pet shop to inspect and ascertain if any offences against Act committed. Must be reasonable time. Obstruction: £500 fine
elines Act	1962	Access pipeline lying across or adjacent to land	HMRC officer may enter land to get to, or leave, any pipeline carrying a dutiable substance which is adjacent to the land

POWERS ALLOWING IMMEDIATE ENTRY, WHERE NO WARRANT IS AVAILABLE

Act Title	Year	Purpose	Form/Requirements
Planning (Listed Buildings and Conservation Areas) Act	1990	Carry out works required by Listed Building Enforcement Notice but not carried out by owner of building	If notice not complied with within time limit set by the notice, local authority may enter the land to carry out the works itself and recover the cost from the owner
Planning (Listed Buildings and Conservation Areas) Act	1990	Inspect to decide whether buildings should be listed, whether being repaired properly, whether enforcement action needed	Must show authority, enter at reasonable time. Must give 24 hours' notice to enter occupied land. Obstruction: £500 fine
Plant Health Act	1967	Inspect for plant disease	Secretary of State or Forestry Commission may issu orders empowering DEFRA officials to enter for purposes specified in the order.
Plant Varieties and Seeds Act	1964	Inspect for compliance with regulations on sale of seeds	Person authorised by secretary of state may enter at any reasonable time any premises where reason to believe seeds being sold, provided not used only as dwelling. Obstruction: £1,000 fine
Poisons Act	1972	Inspect for presence of controlled poisonous substances	Inspector appointed by local authority may enter at a reasonable time to enter premises where reason to suspect breach of law committed, or where person registered to keep poisons carries on business. Obstruction: £500 fine
Police Act	1997	Investigate serious crime	Senior officer of National Crime Squad or National Criminal Intelligence Service (now SOCA), of regular police force or of HMRC may authorise any entry on interference with property or wireless telegraphy to assist in detection or prevention of serious crime whe no other means effective. Where dwelling involved, must have approval of Commissioner (senior judge appointed by govt), unless urgent
Prevention of Damage by Pests Act	1949	Inspect for presence of rats and mice, or compliance with notice requiring extermination; carry out work in default	Person authorised in writing may enter at reasonable time on production of authority. Must give 24 hours' notice to enter occupied land. Obstruction: £200 fine
Protection of Animals Act	1911	Inspect knacker's yard	Constable may enter at any time of day to ascertain compliance with provisions of Act. Obstruction: £200 fine

POWERS ALLOWING IMMEDIATE ENTRY, WHERE NO WARRANT IS AVAILABLE

t Title	Year	Purpose	Form/Requirements
ublic Health Act	1936	Carry out work to cleanse verminous premises	If local authority has served a notice requiring the owner/occupier of verminous premises to cleanse those premises, and such work has not been undertaken, the local authority may enter to carry out the work itself.
efuse Disposal menity) Act	1978	Remove vehicle or other item abandoned on land	Person duly authorised in writing by local authority may enter at any reasonable time after giving 24 hours' notice any "open land" (ie not covered by structure). Must show authority. Obstruction: £500 fine
egional Development encies Act	1998	Survey land with a view to acquiring it or value it for compensation purposes	Must serve 28 days' notice of intended entry. Any authorised official of RDA can then enter land at a reasonable time if he shows evidence of his authority. Obstruction: £1,000 fine
ding Establishments t	1964	Inspect riding establishment	Any person authorised in writing by local authority may enter any premises where horses kept for hire or for instruction for payment. Entry must be at reasonable time. Obstruction: £500 fine
ghts of Way Act	1990	Inspect bridleway or footpath on private land, and/or carry out work to make good the surface	Inserts Schedule 12A into the Highways Act 1980. Must give 24 hours' notice to occupier, unless simply surveying land which is not a building. If occupier unidentified, must attach notice to prominent object. Can then bring men and equipment onto land to carry out work to restore surface.
oad Traffic Act	1988	Inspect goods vehicle	Inspector can enter premises where reason to believe goods vehicle kept in order to inspect the vehicle. Obstruction: £1,000 fine
oad Traffic Regulation t	1984	Maintain road signs	Local traffic authority may enter land to erect/remove/maintain signs
aughter of Poultry Act	1967	Inspect conditions of poultry slaughter	Inspector appointed by local authority or Secretary of State may enter any premises where slaughter in progress or carried out within 48 hours. Obstruction: £500 fine
cial Security ministration Act	1992	Inspect for any evidence of benefit offences, or circumstances of industrial accidents resulting in benefit claims, or investigate whether benefits payable.	Must show authority and enter at reasonable time. Can apply to dwellings if used for business purposes. Obstruction: £1,000 fine

POWERS ALLOWING IMMEDIATE ENTRY, WHERE NO WARRANT IS AVAILABLE

Act Title	Year	Purpose	Form/Requirements
Sunday Trading Act	1994	Check for Sunday Trading offences	Sunday Trading inspector can enter any premises at any reasonable time with or without constable. Must show written authority from Local Authority. Obstruction: £1,000 fine
Taxes Management Act	1970	Capital Gains Tax inspection	Inspector appointed by Board of HMRC may enter to inspect value of property. Not explicit entry power but implied by necessity if property immovable. Obstruction: £200 fine
Taxes Management Act	1970	Determine annual value of land for the purposes of income tax or corporation tax	Inspector appointed by HMRC may enter land at any reasonable time, on showing authority, to inspect and value. No enforcement provisions.
Town and Country Planning Act	1990	Valuations in connection with compensation claims possibly made against local authority over planning restrictions	Authorised officer of local authority may enter on production of authority. Must state his purpose. Must give 24 hours' notice.
Town and Country Planning Act	1990	Survey land in accordance with multiple planning provisions, such as decision on whether to designate unitary development plan etc.	Must show authority, must give 24 hours' notice to enter occupied land. Obstruction: £500 fine.
Transport and Works Act	1992	Erect, inspect, maintain and repair any signage or other fittings connected with railway	Must make reasonable effort to obtain owner's consent, then serve notice. After 42 days, Secretary o State may authorise entry.
Weeds Act	1959	Check for presence of certain specified virulent weeds	Written authorisation from Minister, Must serve notice of date of intended entry on occupier. Obstruction: £1,000 fine
Wildlife and Countryside Act	1981	Various inspection powers related to work of the Nature Conservancy Council	Officer of Nature Conservancy Council may enter at a reasonable time on producing authority and after givin 24 hours' notice. Can be used against private land bu not dwelling. Obstruction: £1,000 fine

TABLE FIVE

POWERS OF ENTRY IN SECONDARY LEGISLATION

.1 Under the European Communities Act 1972

SI Name	Year	Purpose	Remarks
Carriage of Goods (Prohibition of Discrimination) Regulations	1977	Inspect for compliance with European law on carriage of goods	Must produce authority
Hops Certification Regulations	1979	Inspect premises where hops or hop products made, treated, packed or sold	Inspectors appointed by Secretary of State may enter and inspect at reasonable time on production of authority. Obstruction: £1,000 fine
Farm and Horticultural Development Regulations	1981	Inspect land in respect of which agricultural development grant made or claimed	Person authorised by Secretary of State may enter at reasonable time on showing authority
Animal Health Act (Amendment) Regulations	1992	Inspect animal health conditions	Extends use of entry power under AHA 1981 to enforcement of EC obligations
Conservation (Natural Habitats &c.) Regulations	1994	Conservation inspections	Officials of conservation bodies may enter at reasonable time on production of authority. No notice if checking for offence against EC regulations, otherwise 14 hours – 7 days notice depending on purpose. JP can give warrant for constable to enter and search. Obstruction: £1,000 fine
EC Competition Law (Articles 84 and 85) Enforcement Regulations	2001	Inspect for compliance with EC competition rules	Office of Fair Trading officers. Must give 2 working days' notice indicating purpose of investigation, unless reasonable grounds to believe premises occupied by subject of investigation; or unless tried but failed to contact occupier to give notice, in which case must simply show authorisation. JP's warrant can authorise force and immediate entry without notice.
Money Laundering Regulations	2003	Inspect for evidence of money laundering offences	Must have JP's warrant

Animal By-Products Regulations	2005	Inspect for compliance with EC rules on animal by-products	Enter at reasonable hours, must show authority. Must give 24 hours' notice to enter dwelling. EC representative may accompany. Obstruction: £5,000 fine and/or 2 years prison
Animals and Animal Products (Import and Export) (England) Regulations	2006	Inspections related to Common Agricultural Policy.	Must show authorisation. Obstruction: £5,000 fine and/or 3 months prison
EC Fertilisers (England and Wales) Regulations	2006	Supervise fertiliser use	Enter at reasonable hours, must show authority. Must give 24 hours' notice to enter dwelling. EC representative may accompany. JP's warrant can authorise force. Obstruction: £5,000 fine and/or 2 years prison
Products of Animal Origin (Third Country Imports) (England) Regulations	2006	Check for compliance with import controls	Food Standards Agency officer or local authority veterinary or fish inspector may enter at reasonable hours, must show authority. Must give 24 hours' notice to enter dwelling.
Transmissible Spongiform Encephalopathies (No. 2) Regulations	2006	Prevent spread of BSE etc.	Implements EC Regulation 178/2002. Local authority and Secretary of State appoint inspectors. Can enter to ensure Community regulation on TSE complied with. May be accompanied by EC representative. Obstruction: £5,000 fine and/or 2 years prison

5.2 Under the United Nations Act 1946

SI Name	Year	Purpose	Remarks
Libya (United Nations Sanctions) Order	1993	Search for evidence of trade with Libya	Customs officers and constables may enter with JP's warrant. Obstruction is an offence.
Serbia and Montenegro (United Nations Sanctions) Order	1993	Search for evidence of trade with Serbia and Montenegro	Customs officers and constables may enter with JP's warrant. Obstruction is an offence.
United Nations Arms Embargoes (Liberia, Somalia and the Former Yugoslavia) Order	1993	Search for evidence of arms trading with Liberia, Somalia or the former Yugoslavia	Customs officers and constables may enter with JP's warrant. Obstruction is an offence.
Former Yugoslavia (United Nations Sanctions) Order	1994	Search for evidence of trade with the former Yugoslavia	Customs officers and constables may enter with JP's warrant. Obstruction is an offence.

Haiti (United Nations Sanctions) Order	1994	Search for evidence of trade with Haiti	Customs officers and constables may enter with JP's warrant. Obstruction is an offence.
United Nations International Tribunal) (Former Yugoslavia) Order	1996	Search for persons or evidence sought by International Criminal Tribunal for the Former Yugoslavia	JP's warrant authorises a constable in uniform to enter in search of persons or evidence wanted by ICTY
United Nations International Tribunal) (Rwanda) Order	1996	Search for persons and evidence wanted by the International Criminal Tribunal for Rwanda	JP's warrant authorises a constable in uniform to enter in search of persons or evidence wanted by ICTR
Federal Republic of Yugoslavia (United Nations Sanctions) Order	1998	Search for evidence of trade with Federal Republic of Yugoslavia	JP's warrant required. Customs officers and constables may enter. Obstruction is an offence, no penalty specified.
Al-Qa'ida and Taliban (United Nations Measures) Order	2002	Search for evidence of trade with Al-Qa'ida or the Taliban	Customs officers and any constable may enter premises with JP's warrant to search.
Somalia (United Nations Sanctions) Order	2002	Search for evidence of trade with Somalia	Customs officer may enter with any constables with JP's warrant.